ASSISTING RULES!

THE ULTIMATE GUIDE TO ASSISTING MAKEUP ARTISTS AND HAIRSTYLISTS IN BEAUTY, FASHION AND PRINT

ASSISTING
DESHAWN HATCHER RULES!

THE ULTIMATE GUIDE TO ASSISTING MAKEUP ARTISTS AND HAIRSTYLISTS IN BEAUTY, FASHION AND PRINT

FOREWORD BY KEVIN JAMES BENNETT
EMMY AWARD-WINNING MAKEUP ARTIST AND EDUCATOR
AND FOUNDER OF COSMETIC JUNKIE™

**TO ALL MY ASSISTANTS,
THE GOOD, AND THE BAD
YOU'VE ALL MADE ME A BETTER KEY
AND A BETTER PERSON.**

**TO MY GREAT ASSISTANTS,
(AND YOU KNOW WHO YOU ARE)
THANK YOU FOR ALWAYS GETTING
MY LATTES JUST RIGHT.**

In Memoriam
BELINDA KEATTS (1982-2013)

DeShawn Hatcher - ASSISTING RULES!
www.ASSISTINGRULES.com

Book Layout © DeShawn Hatcher
Graphic Designer - Julie Lundy (www.juliekaren.com)

ASSISTING RULES!
The Ultimate Guide to Assisting Makeup Artists & Hairstylists in Beauty, Fashion & Print

This book has been proofed to death. Even the best proofreader will miss something. Any typos are completely unintentional, and when you write your first book I promise not to comment on your typos either :)

SCHOOLS & ORGANIZATIONS
If you would like to order ASSISTING RULES! for your school, please contact us at www.ASSISTINGRULES.com for special sales discounts.

THIS BOOK IS DEDICATED TO

Tommy

Thank you for your
love and support.
This could not have
been written without you.

Love you,

DeShawn

FOREWORD

Thanks to the internet and social media, we have amazing access to information and a huge variety of research tools at our fingertips. Unfortunately, this also allows people with few or no credentials to spread misinformation and call their unverifiable opinions "facts".

DeShawn Hatcher is a beacon of light in these murky waters. A voice of reason, offering no apologies or sugar-coating…just well-researched, factual advice learned the correct way—through *assisting*. She shares how she built her amazing career by taking no shortcuts and learning the inner workings of this industry from the bottom up.

She is thoroughly qualified to break down the assisting process into logical steps and offers real-world advice on how to get the most out of this integral phase of your career.

The creative arts are no different than any other profession—you don't graduate from college and automatically become a CEO. If you want to achieve success and longevity in this industry, you have to start at the beginning, develop your skills, and learn the proper etiquette and protocol.

In an age of entitlement and "Insta-Famous" artists, assisting is deemed distasteful and unnecessary. But it is the fundamental path to learning your craft, if you want this to be your profession, and not a part-time job or hobby.

I've know DeShawn for over a decade and have developed a sincere and deep admiration for her diverse talents. She is a superb makeup artist, an inspiring educator and an extremely articulate writer. But the thing I treasure most about her is our friendship. To say that I'm honored and humbled she asked me to write this Foreword would be a gross understatement.

Thank you, DeShawn, for providing this amazing workbook…and for being my friend.

KEVIN JAMES BENNETT
EMMY AWARD-WINNING MAKEUP ARTIST, AND EDUCATOR,
AND FOUNDER OF COSMETIC JUNKIE

In my life people will come and go, but there are some who, when I think of them, I feel nothing but gratitude and love. I always say, no one can make it alone; there's always people who give of their time and their knowledge. I call them my **MAKEUP ANGELS.**

THANK YOU!

KEVIN JAMES BENNETT

KJB, my two-time-Emmy-Award-Winning friend, to say I simply adore you and cherish our friendship over these many years is an understatement. I am beyond honored and so thankful that you wrote the Foreword to my book. I love you!

FADIL BERISHA

Really, what can I say to someone who saw talent in me, and then nurtured and mentored me and my hard head for years? I'm not sure where I'd be without you; I'm just glad I never have to find out.

SARAH MCCOLGAN

My sister from another Mother, we grew up together in this business. I'm so proud of you and everything you have and will accomplish. I am such a fortunate black gurl that I have you in my life. I love you!

MICHEAL DEVELLIS

You made me an educator for The Powder Group, very early in my career. I cannot tell you what that meant and what it still means to me today, to be in such an esteemed group of artists. I am so honored. Thank you so much, Michael.

JAMES VINCENT

James, you have been nothing but supportive, and just a wonderful person to me throughout my career. Your introductions before the Powder Group classes I'd teach were so heart-warming; I wish I could have framed them all! Thank you.

DYANA AIVES

If it weren't for you, and your brutal and much-appreciated honesty, I would still be writing those obnoxious letters, hahaha! You have no idea how much I have appreciated your tough love and guidance. Thank you so much!

SHAWN LUCAS

I know you hate any kind of accolade—and I don't care. If it weren't for you sharing your knowledge with me, I'd still be sitting behind that desk at ING. There are not enough words to convey my gratitude. Love you!

MARY ERICKSON

I am not sure what I would have done without all of your support and guidance through the rough message board years, lol. It's hard to put my gratitude into words without crying. I'm a mentor because of your example—I just hope I'm half as good as you. Thank you, Mary, I am a blessed black girl for having you in my life.

JANICE AND DENISE TUNNULL

Ladies, what can I say, you two have been supporting me and putting me on your fabulous radio show for years. I am so honored to know you both and so proud to be a part of your show, *Beauty Talk with Illusions*, yes!

JENNA PACE AND HER ASSISTANT, SCOTT

Jenna, you are hands-down the best videographer! You just get me, lady (lol.) I am so grateful for our friendship and cherish it. You know you always have your own personal makeup artist. Scott—you know I adore you!

JULIE LUNDY

This book could not have been done without you. Thanks so much for all your amazing expertise and patience.

SHARON GAULT

You gave me my first assisting gigs 13 years ago; I've never forgotten your kindness, your amazing makeup, and all the lessons I learned. I use what I learned with you in the way I treat my assistants today. I appreciate you, and I thank you.

DEBBIE BONDAR, SIMMY, AND THE WHOLE CREW AT FACE ATELIER

Words cannot express how much I love you guys and appreciate your love and support all these years.

ROLANDO SANTANA

You, my dear, trusted me with all of the beauty for your amazing fashion shows, and now because of you I have an amazing career as a Beauty Director. To the Santana design posse and you all know who you are, "MUAH!" :)—much love.

BARRY BERGER

I loved being in your TV/Film/Print makeup classes at night 14 years ago. I couldn't wait to leave work to get to your class. I loved all the stories you'd tell. I learned so much that I still use to this day. All the folks who have taken your class over the years are very fortunate people. THANK YOU!

WHAT THIS BOOK IS

needs possession

Assistants' or assistant's

THIS BOOK IS THE ANSWER TO ALL ASSISTANTS' DREAMS
—a book to finally give answers to all who

* want to be,

* don't know how to be, or

* are just plain bad at being (because they don't have a clue)

...Makeup Artists' and Hairstylists' Assistants!

WHAT THIS BOOK IS NOT

THIS BOOK IS NOT A HAND-HOLDING, I-WILL-DO-IT-ALL-FOR-YOU BOOK. This book requires action, and asks for input that only you can give. You all are amazing in your own right, each person is different, your goals and your dreams are different. This books speaks to your individuality as if you were in a class setting. It is YOU who will have to do the work. What you'll get out of it is a lifetime of lessons that will surpass assisting and take you into your career as a Key. I am honored to be a part of this journey.

WHAT I KNOW

YOU WILL GET OUT OF THIS BOOK WHAT YOU PUT IN. If you make a commitment, do the homework and learn all the lesson this book has to offer, you will succeed.

DESHAWN HATCHER

AUTHOR OF ASSISTING RULES!

Beauty was always in DeShawn's blood, but growing up, entrepreneurship was unheard of—it was all about getting a job with good pay and benefits. So all of her dreams were put on hold. Then one day her friend Shawn asked her the question that would change her life: "What would you do for free?" The revelation was makeup, and she never looked back. Thirteen years later, after teaching, mentoring and writing for her blog (deshawnlovesmakeuptheblog.com), she decided to help out artists both new and seasoned, yet again, with *ASSISTING RULES!* "My goals in writing *ASSISTING RULES!* are to have artists get the most out of their experience assisting, and for Key artists to stop wishing for better assistants. Assisting is a powerful experience, one that can shape your career for the future, and I want you to be equipped with the truth and answers no one seems to want to say. Assisting can change the trajectory of your life. When you know what to look for it can only make you more aware of the vital lessons to be learned. This book will help you see those lessons and how to parlay them into an amazing career. Don't you want to be great at your job? I know I do!" DeShawn grew up in E. NY, then moved to Rockaway Park, a place recently left in shambles by ~~DeShawn grew up in East New York, Brooklyn then moved to a small town in Queens, NY, Rockaway Park~~ when she was 6—a place recently almost ~~destroyed by~~ Hurricane Sandy. She's a beach girl by way of Brooklyn (That is probably where her tough teacher style comes into play, with her laid back nurturing side that kicks in ~~right~~ when you need it, that has made her a valued mentor and a great educator and friend.)

"I believe everyone in my classes should learn something they didn't know. It's never a one-sided, my way or the highway approach. I love to invite my students to ask me questions, and to engage in conversation. I wrote *ASSISTING RULES!* in that style—I'm talking to you and asking you questions. I'm trying to open dialogue with my readers. "In the past, I've had times when I truly needed to learn, and no one would show me. I'd get a reply like 'I got mine; now you get yours!' or a snap reply like 'Figure it out on your own.' Ain't that a bunch of crap—how the hell can anyone learn that way? And *that* is one reason DeShawn's always teaching and mentoring, and why she has taken a year and a half of her life between fashions shows and photo shoots to write *ASSISTING RULES!*

TABLE OF CONTENTS

DESHAWN HATCHER

PART 1

RESEARCH THE PAST MASTERS / IT'S A PROCESS / HOW WELL DO YOU KNOW THE ARTISTS / AGENCIES ARE DIFFERENT / AGENCIES/ SOCIAL MEDIA / TAKE A CLASS / ~~RESEACHING~~ TRENDS / WHAT THEIR SITE IS TELLING YOU & FORMS *Researching*

MARKETING & PRESENTATION SELF PROMOTION / TELL YOUR STORY / BRANDING / CONNECT TO THE KEY / SET YOURSELF APART WITH TRENDS / LOGICAL WEBSITE AND PORTFO-LIO SET UPS / HOW MANY PHOTOS / WHAT TO DO WHEN YOU ARE NEW / BIO'S / WEBMASTERS / HOW TO ORGANIZE YOUR BOOK / NETWORKING / SOCIAL MEDIA

COMMUNICATION COLD CALLING / HOW TO SET UP A CALL / SCRIPT IT / CORE CONVERSATION / THE WRITE WAY / COVER LETTERS / WHY KEYS DON'T RETURN YOUR EMAILS / SAMPLE LETTERS AND PHONE CALLS / THE CORRECT WAY TO CALL

PART 2

YOU GOT THE GIG! KEY PERSONALITIES / DID YOU LEARN ANYTHING? / TURN RUDNESS AROUND / BEFORE THE GIG / CODE OF ETHICS / SET ETIQUETTE / AFTER THE GIG / TIME FOR AN UPDATE / DON'T BELIEVE THE HYPE / TOO PICKY / SELF ~~ASSESMENT~~ TIME & FORMS *ASSESSMENT*

DESHAWN HATCHER

PART 1

Your work is to discover your world and then with

DESHAWN HATCHER

all your heart give yourself to it.

BUDDAH

01

ANATOMY OF ASSISTING

As a print artist, the work I get covers so many different areas. It has given me opportunities to branch out into many areas of expertise. My work has been on national billboards, international fashion magazines, and music videos. I've been Key for several fashion shows, and Beauty Director with a staff of 80. I'm also a beauty educator, and now even a writer, first with my blog and now with two national magazines. I have built a good celebrity clientele, and so much more. When I think about where I started, I can become dizzy trying to remember it all. I'm just one of many who are privileged to work in this amazing industry. When you assist us, you come work alongside us and learn from industry senior artists.

OPPORTUNITIES ABOUND

Let me shed a huge light on the work that exists in the print world for a makeup artist/hairstylist. You could be assisting on:

PRINT EDITORIAL: National and International Fashion and Beauty Magazines such as *Vogue* and *Pop Marie Claire;* Business publications like *Forbes, Time;* entertainment magazines, *People, US Weekly;* Catalogs from FAO Schwarz to Bloomingdale's.

MUSIC: CD covers from country to classical, hip-hop and alternative, Music videos, musical promo, artist development.

ADVERTISING: from the cover of a hair color box to a Mercedes-Benz car campaign; Billboards, print ads, events, advertorials, live events.

CELEBRITIES / PERSONALITIES / POLITICIANS: including the President of the United States.

FASHION SHOWS: (all levels) corporate, mall, runway shows to the highest level Mercedes-Benz Fashion Week in NY, London, Paris, Milan.

SPECIAL EVENTS: Brides and private engagements, press junkets, pageants, red carpet, cosmetic companies, tours, etc.

What! Do you see what I'm talking about here people? The opportunities for work, with these dynamic master print artists, goes far and beyond the scope of just print. When you apply for an assisting position from a print artist, know you could be working on any of the above at any time.

FREELANCE DOESN'T MEAN FREE

Freelance doesn't mean, "Yes, finally, I am free! I have no rules, and no one to report to." Wrong! No one goes from setting up shop to being a successful CEO overnight. It takes major steps just to reach the role of assistant, and it is so worth it. Assisting is very much like being a college student on an internship, or doing an apprenticeship before joining a union. Assisting is a step you will take in your career of beauty to further your knowledge and become a better artist for the future. The amount of work, effort, and practice you give will dictate what you will get out of your future. The beauty of knowing this is that you can make a clear decision about what path you want to take. To have a promising career, you've got to know what to do and understand ~~clearly and honestly~~ the steps to get there. This book will take you through it all. _clearly._

WHAT DOES AN ASSISTANT DO?

You will provide minute-to-minute assistance on set, and sometimes before a shoot (pre-production) to the Key. Some pre-production duties might be setting up mood boards and gathering supplies. When working on set, some of your tasks are keeping the table organized, maintaining the brushes, getting coffee, running errands, making up models and so much more. When I first started as an assistant, I had to do it all! This included labeling, repacking enormous makeup kits, baby-sitting, errands, nails, hair…and oh yeah… _doing makeup!_

WHAT'S THE BENEFIT?

As an assistant, you get a great insight into the entertainment, fashion, and beauty industry, working alongside professional artists with years of experience. When I assisted, it totally changed the way I did makeup. It improved my timing and my makeup application. When the time came for me to have my assistants and run my team, I was 100% ready to go. It made me ready to be a Key, a good Key, and then a Beauty Director. Assisting is truly an education in sets, photography, models, client diplomacy, production, time management, ~~even~~ how to deal with assistants…and the list goes on. The great assistants know how to use this position to their advantage. They become amazing Keys responsible for some of the hottest editorials, fashion shows and advertisements. Assisting is an avenue where you can start building your career. _But first_, you must know how to go about it.

LOCATION, LOCATION — DON'T BE A LAZY ARTIST

You don't have any artists in your area to assist? Then branch out to other locations. You may have to travel to the nearest major city to find an artist. Don't assume that because you don't come from a place like New York, the opportunities will never happen. I'm a born and raised New Yorker, but I had to travel out of state to get some of my first breaks. ~~So just know this and~~ save your money for the minute the Key calls you with an assisting job. It will be worth your while. This book will guide you to ask the right questions and to jump to the head of the line.

PART OF THE GLAM SQUAD

Many people who want to be a part of this industry want to be close to celebrities. They dream of being a part of the "Glam Squad." Though there is nothing wrong with wanting to glamorize some of the world's most beautiful women, you must remember that you're an *artist* before you become a "*celebrity artist*." Please understand that if you're in it to "hang with celebrities," you're in the wrong business. Don't bother to assist; please just don't bother. Why? Because you're motivated by celebrity and not by being the best assistant you can be. Don't believe all the smoke and mirrors you see on TV. Those artists have paid their dues, and their assistants are very skilled.

WORKING ON SET

Your level of artistry will dictate how far your Key will let you work on set. If you don't know how to do a ponytail or line lips, don't expect to be working on models. What I want you to concentrate on is your job. There will be tons of things for you to learn, and ~~tons of things for you to~~ do. Don't feel that if you don't ~~get the chance to~~ work on a model, you accomplished nothing that day. First of all, *you actually got on set!* That is a major accomplishment! Secondly, you will learn amazing techniques and tricks along the way that can only help you in your artistry. Just because you are a seasoned artist doesn't mean you'll be working on models, either. ~~Just~~ keep in mind that you are there to assist. If you want to work on models, you had better learn what your Key actually does. This book will show you how to do exactly that.

HOW MUCH CAN I MAKE?

Most assisting gigs start out unpaid for inexperienced artists. Working editorials are notorious for this. Assisting works as a barter. I give you access to information, and you work for me for a day for free. Pay is at the discretion of the Key—no two Keys pay the same.

TIME AND COMMITMENT
DO YOU HAVE THE TIME?

Do you have kids, a hubby, a job? Can you work for free? Will your partner understand long hours and no pay? Sometimes you can be on set for 12 or more hours. Can you deal with that with children? Having the time is as important as being able to afford to work for free. You may have to assist on a part-time basis, and that's OK. The route may be a bit slower for you to become the artist you want to be, but you've got to hang in there. With determination and strategy, you will be able to work it out.

YOUR SKILL LEVEL

Assisting doesn't require a Ph.D. in makeup or hair-ology. We know you are assisting to obtain knowledge that will help you in becoming a phenomenal working artist on your own. When we're assessing your skill, we all know you haven't worked for *Vogue*...so *relax!* Understand that there are so many variables that go into being a great assistant. What skills do you possess that can make a Key's day run smoothly? Different Keys look for different things in their assistants, so don't be concerned if you don't have the greatest makeup or hair skills; it could be your great people skills we need. If you are a seasoned artist, make sure when asked you can perform the task extremely well.

HOW LONG MUST I ASSIST?

How long you assist is clearly up to you. You may not like it. You can assist once and never want to do it again. No two Keys (lead artists) are the same, so your experiences will not be the same. I would suggest to try it at least three times with different people and different jobs. Don't let one bad experience cloud your judgment. There is too much to gain.

"Assisting goes beyond learning makeup tips. It gives you an incredible opportunity to learn on set etiquette and see the dynamics of a photoshoot."

VIKTORIJA BOWERS ADAMS

THE EXCHANGE

An email, an exchange of your business card, a personal introduction (at a trade show) does not guarantee you go to the front of the line. It doesn't entitle you to a front row seat to the artist. It means you've made contact—that's it. It doesn't entitle you to a timely reply, or any reply at all. It is up to YOU to cultivate that relationship over time. This book tells you how to go about reaching out to artists, and make a connection that only you can.

WHY ASSISTING JOBS ARE SO HARD TO COME BY

The biggest problem is how newbies reach out to senior artists. Unfortunately, many who enter this field seem to think business protocols are not needed. When they inquire about assisting, it is all in the wrong ways —the seniors will not hire them. That's why I'm writing this book. I cannot tell you how many emails I get from entitled newbies with improper spelling, Ebonics, etc. You will not be hired when inquiring in the wrong way.

The number of new artists is over-saturating today's beauty market. There are more artists wanting to assist now than ever before. According to BeautySchoolsDirectory.com, there are 40 beauty schools in New York state, and 15 just in NYC. On the west coast, there are a whopping 90 beauty schools pumping out artists. Don't forget to figure in all the workshops and self-proclaimed artists out there.

When I started in NY about 13 years ago, there were approximately 4 "Beauty schools" in NYC and only one with a certified class in Print/TV/Film. Now, keep in mind how many "working" professionals/senior artists there really are, and perhaps the picture is a little clearer. The opportunities for assisting can be hard to come by because the supply just isn't there. Knowing the ins and outs of the field will give you an advantage over others that haven't a clue.

Another reason why assisting jobs are so hard to come by is simply because of Keys' previous bad experiences with assistants. I am sure many of the senior artists have stories about how an assistant went behind their back to steal their clients, or was just horrible to work with. Really, I can go on.

it's

Assisting is a skill, but ~~its~~ also a very personal relationship. Assistants come into our homes, can meet our families, know our personal business, etc. Unfortunately, there can be people who take advantage of this relationship. I've had some severely shady assistants, and when it happens it can seriously knock you off your feet. It can make an artist leery of even thinking about getting a new assistant. These sneaky, backstabbing people truly make it harder for you to be the *next* assistant.

Please adhere to the guidelines outlined in this book! I promise you that the information you find here will help you to become an amazing *assistant* and then an amazing *artist*.

MENTORSHIP

I am always amazed when I hear artists say, "Oh, I don't want to assist; I just want a mentor." When a Key becomes interested in training you and mentoring you, that relationship goes far beyond assisting. I have been a mentor to many artists over the years, but I have also *stopped* mentoring people who show no commitment to the craft or the business. Mentoring is by far the most time-consuming extracurricular activity a Key artist can do for an assistant. Mentoring happens in a relationship and is not to be taken lightly. It does not happen overnight. We will only mentor assistants who show a hunger, passion and dedication for the business and the craft. Mentorship does not happen because you simply ask for it. Understand that the process of mentoring is only for the most dedicated artists.

The hardest part about starting a new journey is the

beginning. Once you take that first step, you're on your way.

DESHAWN HATCHER

RE
SEA

DESHAWN HATCHER

R
CH

02

THE PAST IS YOUR PRESENT

You have to know the industry you are entering. It is imperative. We all speak about past artists and their work, and we all pay homage to them in one way or another. Why? It shows we know what came before us, it have shows a clear understanding of what the industry is at large, and it will show you that no artist is really all that original, but all the masters are amazing. If you know names like Gucci, Prada, Valentino, then you must know names like Fine, Aucoin, Brown, McGrath, Garren, Sasson, and Pita. You cannot know where it is you're heading until you know where your passion comes from. Researching the past master artists will be the first step to help you lay the foundation for an amazing career. You will see how the artists of today emulate their styles. Your research into the past will give you a deeper appreciation of the techniques and aspirations of the artists of today.

A DESHAWN STORY

A few years ago, I was at the Makeup Show, at the Kevyn Aucoin booth. I do this every time I am there; I go to his booth to silently pay my respects to an artist that means the world to me. I was standing next to two newbies who were elated to finally be at this booth. They were talking about how much they love Kevyn and his work. How they wanted to work for his company and so on. You would have thought I was backstage at a concert—these two were just going on and on…it was sweet.

When the gentlemen behind the counter walked over to help them, they explained their love for all things Kevyn. This too was lovely—until they asked the gentleman if he was Kevyn.

I tried to hide my expression, but people, my jaw was wide open. The nice gentleman's eyes locked with mine for a moment, and he turned to the girls and said nicely, "Well, no, I'm not Kevyn. Kevyn Aucoin passed away over nine years ago."

Do you think those ladies stood a chance at working for the company? THEY LEFT EMBARRASSED! And so they should have. If you don't know who came before, chances are you will be LEFT BEHIND. You really don't want to look like a fool in front of someone, you should *know*.

The only way for this not to happen is—you guessed it!—RESEARCH.

Know your past! How much time would it have taken to do a search on Kevyn? Maybe two seconds! You've got to quit just looking at the pretty pictures, and start learning what is really important: the artists behind the pictures.

I want you to go to the web and research the Masters I have listed in the coming section and beyond. I want you to get inspired and get to know their individual styles, and get to know their stories. When you do, you'll be amazed, because so many of these Masters assisted other great artists, too.

MAKEUP MASTERS

The following artists have all been in the business for well over 20 years. They are know as the iconic artists of our time. Reseach all of them!

SAM FINE

This amazing, iconic, legendary artist has blessed the faces of African-American women with his talent for the better part of two decades. I could tell you all the people he has worked with, but that would take me a day. I could then tell you all the people he *hasn't* worked with, but I'm not sure that list exists. No one does a black woman's face like Sam Fine. Get to know this amazing makeup artist. This amazing DVD *The Basics of Beauty* is fabulous for beginners available on Amazon.

VIDAL SASSOON

I am not sure how to convey what this hairstylist legend has done for women all over the world with his precision cuts and funky angles. He turned the hair world upside down in the 60s, and his style is still prevalent today. He continues, even after his passing (in 2010 at the age of 84) to be at the forefront of what we all look like today. It is imperative that you research the amazing Vidal Sassoon. You can view this amazing documentary on Netflix.

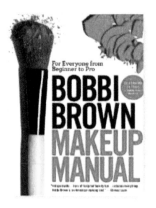

BOBBI BROWN

She's not only a makeup artist, she's a powerhouse business mogul in the world of cosmetics. Her company is worth a billion dollars; her looks can be seen on runways, the first lady, and the hottest celebrities across the globe. Her amazing books that help everyday woman with their makeup applications should definitely be in your library. She is a true inspiration for all makeup artists.

KEVYN AUCOIN

Kevyn Aucoin has a special place in my heart. I wanted to be a makeup artist after seeing his work and reading all his books. He inspired me to be where I am today. There is so much to be said about Kevyn Aucoin, that this book cannot contain everything. His magic was used on the hottest fashion runways, on the original Supermodels. He did makeup for Janet Jackson, Jennifer Lopez, Tina Turner, and so many others. His skill to transform women is documented in his books *Making Faces* and *Face Forward*. Before his death, he created his signature Kevyn Aucoin Cosmetics, which is a staple in makeup artists' kits today.

SERGE NORMANT

Another legend of the hair world's craft can be seen on some of the hottest women of today. Serge Normant's career spans over 30 years and he is still making women's manes ferocious. Just look up the shoot he did with Julia Roberts—talk about gorgeous, full hair! That look was repeated in many fashion and beauty editorials—even in some of mine. Big hair was the rage all because of this legend.

MARIETTA CARTER NARCISSE

Marietta is one of the few Black makeup department heads in the film and television industry today. Her career rose while working with Spike Lee on many film projects including the classic *Do the Right Thing* and *Malcolm X*. She was the makeup artist working with Whoopie Goldberg on her Oscar-winning film, *Ghost*. One of her latest projects was as department head and Key for the Whitney Houston Story. She's an icon, and her makeup is now being taught across the country. She created the most have *Makeup Planner*, a list of all the upcoming events in our industry. See more at www.MariettaCarter-Narcisse.com.

JOANNE GAIR

Her work literally disappears into the background [painters] because she is one of the premier body painting artists of all time. This amazing New Zealander has taken the beauty business by storm with her artistry. She is behind some of the most famous body painting images you will see in magazines. You must check out Joanna Gair.

FRANCES TOLOT

When you go to Frances Tolot's website, your jaw will drop. She has created some of the amazing looks you have seen on people like Beyonce, Madonna, and Jennifer Lopez. She's a sought-after editorial, advertising, [and] celebrity makeup artist. The book, *One Woman 100 Faces*, is a lesson in transformative makeup.

LISA ELDRIDGE [hate it]

This amazing artist hails from England by way of her native homeland, New Zealand. Though I had seen her work for years in many of my fashion magazines, I was reintroduced to her on YouTube. She is one of the few artists I'd ever recommend learning from on YouTube. Watching her videos and listening to her calm voice is so pleasant; I could watch her all day. She is currently the Global Creative Makeup Director for Lancome. Her book, *Face Paint: The Story of Makeup* will be availabe Oct 2015. [october]

RAE MORRIS

Rae Morris hails from my best friend's homeland of Australia. She is an amazing editorial and celebrity makeup artist. Her many books have been a mainstay for consumers and pros and should be on your bookshelves.

GUIDO

Iconic Hairstylist Guido Palau was a major force behind the grunge movement of the mid-'90s, and today, Guido is described by British *Vogue* as "The World's most in-demand hair stylist." His work is regularly featured in Italian, French, British and American *Vogue, Love, V,* and *W United Magazine.* Each season, he creates the hair look for more than 30 fashion shows. Guido has become one of the busiest runway stylists in the business. His book is simply called *Hair : Guido.*

Francois

~~FRANCIOS~~ NARS

We've all heard of NARS Cosmetics, right? Well, this iconic makeup artist changes the game with his signature styles. Explore the world of NARS though his makeup line and books. *Makeup Your Mind: Express Yourself* is cleverly done and a fun way to learn from one of the makeup industry's leaders.

OTHER NAMES FOR YOUR RESEARCH

Dick Page, Orlando Pita, Kubuki, Reggie Wells, Laura Mercier, Ted Gibson, Pat McGrath, Oscar Blandi, Charlotte Weller, Kevin Woon, Garren, Diane Kendal, Gucci Westman, Peter Philips, Leslie Lopez, Ricky Wilson, Billy B, The Westmores, Brigette Reiss Andersen

MASTER ARTIST RESEARCH FORM

WHAT DID YOU FIND?

Name of the master artist you admire:

Name some other people they have worked with (such as photographers, stylists, etc.)

How did the artist get started in the industry?

What is this artist's specialty, in your opinion?

Where has this artist been featured? List below.

Publications:

What work did you recognize?

Films:

What work moved you?

Music videos:

What were the artist's latest/or last works?

Advertisements:

ANSWER THESE SAME QUESTIONS FOR EACH ARTIST YOU HAVE RESEARCHED. When you do, you will find commonalities and parallels to ~~between~~ your life. Researching isn't simply list-making, ~~it~~ it's done so ~~that you can connect~~ ~~your own~~ style ~~to~~ and the styles of ~~these~~ master artists. Research shows you that you are not alone. For every step you take, someone else took that same journey, ~~and they~~ survived and thrived. Make that connection and I promise, it will only enlighten you! **TO ME THE WORDS "MASTER", "ICON", AND "LEGEND" ARE ALL ATTRIBUTED TO THESE ARTISTS.** I want you to research ~~these amazing artists.~~ then. I want you to be inspired, wowed, and "clutching your pearls" when you see their work.

03

WHAT'S YOUR PASSION?

Research is essential to becoming an assistant; it's essential for anything you want to do in this business. Knowing your passion is ~~also~~ important, because then you know where and ^how ~~what~~ you should concentrate your time. Arm yourself with the knowledge of what the Key/Agency does. Why would you approach an artist for a job and not feel passionate about their work? Why would you approach an artist for a job and not understand their style? If you are going to ask for a job, you should know what job you're asking for and from whom. Don't reach out to an artist or an agency until you have done your homework.

FOCUS: A CHILD'S GAME

Have you ever heard of the children's game "pin the tail on the donkey?" *he* *has*
You know, you blindfold the child, spin him around a few times, and he's
supposed to be able to locate the tail of the donkey on the photo and pin it
on. That's how I feel a lot of you approach trying to find assisting jobs. You
blindly try to pin yourself to any Key just to get a job. What the child who
wins this game knows, is that you must focus on the result and approach the
donkey with a plan in mind. That child has a laser focus on where he wants
to pin the tail, and never loses sight of it, even when blindfolded.

The same process goes for you when it comes to assisting. I bet you didn't
know how strategic "pin the tail" was, did you, lol? I want you to be strategic
with how you go about landing your assisting gigs. No more sending out endless emails saying you want to assist without knowing the Key and their work.

WHAT'S YOUR PASSION?

What is the style of makeup and hair you currently do? Is that the type of
artist and style you want to assist, or would you rather go against that and try
something radical and cool? Here's your chance! Assisting will allow you to
see the other side. If your dream makeup is very funky, artistic and abstract
like artists Alex Box, Elias Faas, and Pat McGrath, then you know you are
more attracted to the more avant garde artist. Maybe you like to work magic
on women of color, like Sam Fine or Reggie Wells. Do you drool over the
big hair of Julia Roberts created by Normant, or dream of the precision cuts
of the incredible, pioneering, late, great hairstylist Vidal Sasson? Once you
narrow it down, you can begin the process of becoming an amazing assistant.
You must know where you want to end before you can know where to start.
I call this assisting with a purpose.

WANT TO FIND YOUR PASSION?
HERE'S THE EQUIPMENT NEEDED:

* NOTEBOOK/JOURNAL

* A PEN,

* A COMPUTER (w/ internet access)

* A PRINTER

(YES, THAT'S IT!)

RESEARCH: IT'S A PROCESS

You've got to make a commitment of time when you're working through your researching; you must stay vigilant and ~~persevere~~ *persevere*. Set aside at least half an hour a day ~~to devote~~ to researching artists. When I started, there was slow internet, and sub-par information and search tools. Google wasn't even around, and that was just 13 years ago. At night after work, I'd spend up to 8 hours to do my research, because the internet was faster at night, and I could concentrate. Then off to work I would go the next morning.

I would offer my services as an assistant, or ask for critiques and direction from senior artists. I answered every request for ~~an~~ assistants from artists I'd admired that I could find, and I didn't give up when I didn't get an answer. I also took time to research makeup looks (which is something I still do), as well as to learn more about photographers, art, and more. I bought books and studied all I could about beauty, consulted with photographers, stylists, and hair stylists. ~~You see,~~ while I was waiting for the call, it was my job to do all I could to make myself accessible and skilled.

After six months, one of my emails had gotten through to makeup artist Sharon Gault, and I got THE CALL to assist, and I have never looked back.

All of this was done while I worked on-set for 12 hours, barely slept, barely ate, but I accomplished it. You must be driven and bring all your passion to this process in order to succeed, or you will fade out before you begin. I'm writing this book because I want you to get that assisting gig that can set your career in motion. I want you to know what it's like to work on editorials and then see your work in magazines and so much more. All of this can begin with assisting. You cannot make the declaration that you are a professional artist and qualified to assist, and then put no time or effort into what the industry has to offer. You get back what you put in. There wasn't a day that I didn't practice some new technique, or work to master the ones I already ~~learned~~ *knew*, or do my research.

We are in an age of advanced technology. We can speak into our phones, and information is revealed. So don't tell me you can't do the research. Try doing research without Google—*oy vey!* When you get the job is not the time for you to learn, it's time for you to DO what you have *already* learned.

I want you to be equipped with the right answers when approaching artists/ agencies, because only then will they take you seriously. Let's begin.

"When I consider an assistant, I look for someone who has common sense, who can think outside of the box."

SIAN RICHARDS

HOW WELL DO YOU KNOW THE ARTIST?

How well do you know your favorite, Michael Jackson song? I bet you know every single word and even all the "he-hes." So why don't you know the person you want to assist that well? Now, when I mean "know" them, I don't mean that in a stalker kind of way. I mean, what are their last few editorials, their last print jobs? Do you know their style, their field of expertise?

Assisting requires you to know the artist's work. I'm contacted by newbies who don't have a clue as to the type of makeup I do. They may have seen one image on Facebook or in a magazine, and then they contacted me. Though it's nice to get compliments, and all are appreciated, why don't you look at my site to read my bio and resume? Do you even know that I work on other styles of makeup, projects, or events?

A common complaint I hear from friends who are Keys is that they are approached by uninformed artists for assisting gigs. They cannot understand why they are constantly contacted by artists seeking assisting jobs, who don't have a clue who they are as artists. Do your homework! Your research is the first and most important step to begin the process of knowing the artist. When you take the time to acquire all the information you need, you will be well versed in that artist's style, and on your way.

Case in point:
What happens if the artist gives you the job and now you've got to do makeup their way? Did you study what they do? If they say "I like her to look clean," do you understand? "Clean" means different things to different artists!

Can you ~~image~~ _imagine_ being on set?

Key   *Can you do that model clean for me?*

You   Do you mean, like the look I saw on your site when you did that _Elle_ Magazine spread with Zoe Saldana?

Key   Yes, exactly.

You   Why yes, I can!

What? **Done!** **Ding!** Honey, you would be so in.

Now that's what we're looking for, someone who does their homework! You've got to do your research in order to be impressive.

WHAT THEIR SITE IS REALLY TELLING YOU

When you look at a site, there is loads of information, not just bio details or a resume. This is the kind of information you should be looking for:

* The artist works on various skin tones—do you?

* The artist uses color often—is your color theory up to par?

* Instead of high fashion shoots, the artist works on a lot more commercial brands like, Sears. Is that what you want to do?

* The artist does various makeup styles, from clean to avant-garde—can you help with all of this?

* The artist works on male models—do you know how?

* The artist shoots with a particular team repeatedly. Do you know who the photographer, fashion stylist, makeup artists, and hairstylists are? You may need to research them as well.

Do you get it? Do you see why researching and reviewing their sites from a "How can I help you?" kind of way is so important? You're gathering the information you need to be able to offer your skills. It will give you insight as to what you will be opening yourself up to. After your research, you may find that the artist has more commercial and less high fashion editorial work then you thought. Do you still want to work with them? If not, you just saved yourself from going after that artist. Please know that artists will post provocative work on social media, and those images can make you drool, but that doesn't mean that that is their primary source of work. If you don't investigate, you could find yourself disappointed.

All of this information can be gathered in 5 to 10 minutes, depending on how large an artist's site is. Do you see what you can gather in minutes? Unfortunately, so many newbies/artists just don't take the time.

Seasoned artists don't know what to look for either. Your desire to assist should come with a desire to put in the work and discover the artists. You will gather the information you need to make a better decision, and look for a way for you to "fit" into what that artist does.

If you have to jump on a Facebook group or artist forum to ask what to do because you accepted a paid job,

DESHAWN HATCHER

then you're not a makeup artist.... you're a con artist!

True artists are paid for their skills.

CANDACE COREY

AGENCIES: WHAT'S THE DIFFERENCE?

Agencies have a history. By researching, you will see they all have a story. They have their styles and artists rosters that set them apart from each other. If you ever research agencies (I do all the time), you will see each one has a relationship with various advertisers, magazines, celebrities, etc. If you are an artist who is ready to approach them, you will understand how you could fit into their assistants' roster by studying what it is they do, and what artists are represented by their agency. It will give you references to the types of work you should be striving to achieve and what kind of assisting you will be doing.

For example, Jed Root is different from Exclusive Artists. Jed Root has an international roster, located internationally. They have a huge celebrity clientele, but also high-end, high fashion international magazines and advertising: *Vogue Italia, W magazines, Citizen Kane,* etc. You won't find Sears in this agency. Some of their artists are stars, like the fabulous hairstylist Ted Gibson and amazing makeup artists Laura Mercier and Dick Page.

Exclusive Artists, located in NY and LA, is more celebrity-driven. They are very event/red carpet focused, with an emphasis on celebrity editorials. They have the amazing makeup artist Nick Barose, who has been beautifying some of the hottest actresses in the world, including Oscar winner Lupita N'yongo.

You see, they are both agencies, but they have two different agendas and different styles. Both have amazing artists. Both have fabulous magazines, advertising campaigns, and celebrity clientele. And both of them I am personally obsessed with, lol.

You will find some agencies that are celebrity-focused, some that work with commercial clients, some that are editorial driven, etc. They all have their agenda, and you must find out what that is before approaching them.

WE CAN READ BETWEEN THE LINES

You know how a fortune teller can read your palm and your whole life is revealed? That is very similar to how a Key/Agent can dissect your work. When you present your work for review, Keys can see a myriad of things. We can see if you understand bone structure, contouring, highlighting, color theory, weaves, blow-outs, and up-dos. Keys can tell if you understand what's appropriate for a specific face shape, etc.

We can see if you know what a quality photo shoot is by the other team members' contributions. We are also looking at "post-work" meaning, how well is your work photoshopped. (BTW: over-photoshopping can be as deadly as bad makeup and hair).

We are not just looking at the pretty coral lip, or the amazing way you flat iron hair. We look at the whole picture, the sum of its parts. We do not ignore bad nails, bad models, poor application or bad composition. When you want to approach an agency or artist, be prepared to show your very best work. In this case, quality is much more important than quantity.

RESEARCH THE TEAM AS WELL AS THE ARTIST

You not only research the agency, but you must look through all of the artists on their roster—YES, every single one, including photographers and nail techs. When you do, you will see repeated images from editorials in each artist's portfolio, and those images can tell you who worked on each particular shoot.

You will be able to find out who the team members are and be prepared to work alongside them. No, you're not there to assist them, but knowing the key players is always a benefit to you. Researching the team is a must. Read their bios, methodically go through their work, and then go research them further by looking at their personal websites.

All this must be done before you type out your first introductory email, because you may be assisting on set with them someday. When you apply for an assisting position in an agency, that list can be available to all the artists within the agency, not just the artist you want to assist. It also gives you insight about an artist's working relationships. In your letter to them, you can say something like: "I loved the editorial for Vogue you did with fellow hairstylist Enrique. The makeup (be specific) was beautiful." Comments like these are the "something extra" artists will not expect. I know I wouldn't.

When we can, we tend to like to work with the same team members as much as possible. Not doing your homework can be disastrous.

A DESHAWN STORY

I had an assistant who got to set super early and eager to start her day—fabulous. She did what she was supposed to: called me when she arrived, set up—all great. What she didn't know was that one of the "crew" was the photographer, and she was very rude to him when she arrived. Had she done her homework, she would have known that I shoot with this person a lot. She could have learned who he was, and found out what he looked like. Of course, I was informed of her rude behavior, and she was fired.

Research, people!

TAKE A CLASS

Many Key artists teach. So, why aren't you in class? Classes are one of the greatest ways for you to get to know the Key, and for them to get to know you. They get to see how well you do makeup/hair, how you are as a person, and how well you listen to instruction. Remember, assisting isn't the place for lessons, it is a job and must be respected. I've been so fortunate to acquire several of my assistants through my classes, and they have gone on to work with me on so many high-level paid projects. So, why don't you ever take the classes when offered?

I've had would-be assistants say to me "Oh, I saw that you were teaching, but I figured I would be your assistant, and wouldn't have to pay to learn from you." Really? Those people just lost out.

When you're looking into taking a class from an educator, see how large the classes are, how long they are, and—of course—if it is something that interests you. Classes are the best way to spend time in front of the Key, and for them to get to know you. You can then follow up with them after the class is over. If you've made a great impression, they will remember you. You, my dear, have just gotten yourself noticed.

Remember, this is a business based on personalities. It's vital that the Key get to know you, and what better way then a class? And, by the way, you learn a few things in the process.

BLOGS: WHY DON'T YOU READ THEM?

I want to make this point short and sweet. Research the artist, and find out if they have a blog. If they do, READ IT AND SUBSCRIBE. Many senior artists have blogs. I have had one for five years: deshawnlovesmakeuptheblog.com. My blog's focus is the business, and not so much the products. It is through an artist's blog that you can get a more personal feel for the artist.

We may discuss the industry trends, current and past jobs, artists we admire, the latest works we have done, even give tips and techniques we used to create the looks, and so much more. Some blogs allow you to leave comments and ask questions. Don't miss out on this vital part of researching, because you will be missing a lot.

Most importantly, don't forget to join/subscribe to the artist's blog to show your support. Be vocal if you like something you've read or seen. Artists do remember who supports them.

Currently, more and more agencies are using blogs to feature their artists' latest work. These are amazing, because they will tell you what the artist did, who they worked on, and for what event. Agency Blogs are a wonderful source of information, and should be just as mandatory for your research as artists' blogs.

SOCIAL MEDIA (FACEBOOK/INSTAGRAM/YOUTUBE)

This is not the place to "ask" for a job. If you need a critique on your work, you must approach the artists in the most professional way possible. I strongly suggest you email them directly and not approach them with a "Hey, can you take a look at my Facebook page and tell me what you think?"

The more unprofessional you are, the less likely it is that anyone will take you seriously. I have deleted artists from my friends list who reach out to me unprofessionally on Facebook. What these social media havens are great for is getting a better understanding of the artists. You get a glimpse into their lives, their jobs, and their friends as artists. Like on a blog, social media contains a ton of helpful information. Some artists update their social media page the day of a shoot—hell, some update even while they're working. It's a visual diary for you to see what that artist is about.

You must check all of the social media platforms. For example, some artists may be more visible on Instagram than on Facebook. But alwasys remember, just because these places have a relaxed feel, it doesn't mean you are to approach a Key in a relaxed manner.

RESEARCHING THE TRENDS

When I crossed over from film to the beauty/editorial industry, I was a very good makeup artist, but I wasn't immersed in knowing the trends. In fact, I was a bit of a snob when it came to knowing the latest lipstick shade. I concentrated on my application and technique, and less on celebrities' latest lipstick colors. I was wrong!

When you become a beauty artist, one of your jobs is to know the next season's colors, to research, and not only know what is current, but what will be trendy in the future. When you assist on editorials, you could be witnessing the hottest trend to come. You see, the fabulous fashion shows of NY, Paris, Milan, and beyond all set the trends, they and forecast what the next season's hottest colors and hair trends will be, and how they will be used. If you don't know this, you will be left behind.

Why is it when you see a red lip on the runways, you begin to see it on the covers of magazines, on your favorite stars, and suddenly everywhere? It's a trend. Be informed and be aware of what your industry is doing. You don't want to be asked in an interview what the latest trends are, and not know the answer.

Some of my favorite trend-spotting sites are Harper's Bazaar, Vogue, ~~blog,~~ In the Gloss, Style.com and Pantone.com Pantone is the color company that lets us all know what the next hottest colors will be. How many times did you hear the words Radiant Orchid a few seasons ago? Well, that was thanks to Pantone. They set the color trends for fashion and home decor, and they are even the folks behind the colors in your computer. From these sources you will find tons of beauty looks from the past and present run-way shows all around the world.

"Always be aware of your surroundings and remember, you are there to learn and grow, not to make contacts or get ahead."

LOTTIE

ARTIST INFORMATION FORM

Artist name

Twitter

Website

YouTube

Email address

Phone number

Personal blog
(Don't forget to subscribe!)

Date of introduction

Agency

Facebook

Dates of follow-ups

Instagram

What inspired you? *(Keep any photos you loved on file.)*

Write down everything you see they do. *(Grooming, women, children, commercial, high fashion, portraits, business, women of color, editorials, advertising/ fashion shows/special events, etc)*

What projects do they work on that you can see yourself being a part of? Write it down, be specific:

After reviewing their site, what can you do to help them? *(Ex. Are you great at male grooming, or updos?)* List your related skills below.

Do you have related work that you can show?
☐ Yes ☐ No

Think of your perfect assisting job. What would you like to work on? (Beauty, high fashion, celebrity) or ~~you don't care, you~~ just want experi-ence?) *do you*

What kind of artist would you like to work with? (Conceptual, high fashion, commercial...or ~~you don't care,~~ you just want to do it all?) *do*

Write down all the agencies you want to partner with.

Write down which artist on each agency's roster you'd like to assist.

Write down all the artists you found in the genre you want to work with.

(Remember, when researching artists, you're looking for commonalities. You want to make a genuine connection.)

Does anything on the artist's social media page differ from what you see on their site? If so, write it down.
☐ Yes ☐ No

Does the artist have any special interest projects? If so, list them below.
☐ Yes ☐ No

Do they work with the homeless, cancer patients, do gallery showings etc.? If so, write it down.
☐ Yes ☐ No

Did you find additional press, blog articles, video interviews with the artist, etc. Did you learn anything new about them? If so, what?
☐ Yes ☐ No

Did you do an internet search? Below, record any additional information you've come across that is of interest to you.
☐ Yes ☐ No

This year I am choosing to live beyond my wildest dreams.

I wonder where they'll take me.

OPRAH

MAR
KE

DESHAWN HATCHER

T
ING

04

SELF PROMOTION

Marketing is the most tangible tool you have in getting your business off the ground. Marketing your services to promote yourself as an amazing, invaluable assistant is paramount. Keys and agencies can get a clear understanding of who you are and what you do at a glance. If you have made the declarative statements "I AM A MAKEUP ARTIST" or "I AM A HAIRSTYLIST" and/or "I WANT TO ASSIST" then you must present your most professional side. Anything less screams amateur, and I'm sorry to tell you, but you won't be perceived as a serious candidate when applying for jobs. And people, I want you to get that job!

TELL YOUR STORY

Let me break this down for you,
MARKETING SHOULD ANSWER THESE QUESTIONS.

* Who are you as an artist and as a person?

* What do you bring to the job?

* How can you fit into what the Key/Agency needs?

* What can you do to make yourself invaluable?

It's very much like the format a journalist uses to put together a story. YOU'VE got a story to tell! Get all the particulars in place to make it clear to the artists and agencies that you are the right assistant for the job.

You are here to sell *yourself* first and *your services* second. What makes a story interesting to you is when you can relate to it, right? Make yourself relatable. Through your research, you find out more about the Key/Agency and this will allow you to make yourself "relatable" to the artists and more likely to land the position you seek. You've got to remember this: you're contacting artists who may not have even asked for an assistant. Your marketing is the first line of introduction. It will be your individual form of expression and communication into your professional career. Through marketing, you will begin to answer those questions and so much more.

KNOW YOURSELF: BRANDING

For the longest time, I struggled with marketing and branding. I'd always say, "What makes me so different? I'm just a makeup artist like everyone else." Until a hairstylist friend of mine pointed out that no two makeup artists are the same. We are all originals, just by the simple fact that we are artists.

He pointed out how well I get along with everyone, and how genuine and sincere I am. He listed how professional and respectful I am, how organized I am, how great I am in a crisis, and how I use my humor to make the day easier. He reminded me how I give my time to newbies who need guidance and the truth. "You're more than 'just a makeup artist' DeShawn. What makes a great makeup artist is so much more than just how well you paint a face."

People, I was blown away. I never looked at it that way. We are all made up of parts and within those parts is what makes us all different. Think of that when you are assessing what you bring to the job.

SELF-BRANDING

Self-branding is not so simple. You've got to sit down and figure out what it is that you do best, what it is that people "perceive" that you do best and will pay for, and then evaluate from there. Ask friends, colleagues, and clients what they feel are your best and worst traits.

It's all about the reputation that you build for yourself, throughout your career, that will help you in your branding. Everyone uses examples about different companies; I will too. Think about a company like McDonald's. Now, I ask you, What does McDonald's sell? If you said "burgers", you're wrong! I can hear you now, saying "HUH?" lol. McDonald's sells HAPPINESS. Let's examine this: before the heavy competition (Chuck E Cheese), they were the leaders in all things happy. You could take your kids to McDonald's, and they could play all day in the playground—and that makes them what? HAPPY. The mothers could breathe and take a break, and that made them what? YES! Happy. The meal McDonald's serves their children is a what? Say it with me, a "HAPPY MEAL"! YES! Now you know, there's nothing but over processed foods in that cute little box, but it makes both mom and child—YES!!! Say it with me people! HAPPY!

Let's look at our girl, Oprah. Can we be real here? Was she "this" Oprah, 25 years ago? Ah-a-hell NO, she wasn't. It took her years to build her brand. Her brand is "TRUST." You trust in who she invites on her show, the products she is pushing, and the philosophies she wants to impart. She is a billionaire who can speak to the so-called "average" woman as if she were living in their neighborhood. Millions of women and men TRUST OPRAH. Why? Because she developed the way to connect to every man, women, and child. It took her well over two decades to do it.

So, I say it again and again, branding is not about just putting your face on your card. It's about letting people in on who you are, and how fabulous you are at your business. They have to understand the "perceived value" of your services, or else they won't pay for them. The same thing goes when you are marketing yourself for an assisting job. I've got to figure out by what you're telling if you are "worth" the job. I have to find you of value. Do you understand? If you come across like a complete idiot, who can't follow instructions, doesn't possess any common sense, could embarrass me (or worse, cost me a client), do you think you would be my assistant?. Ah-aHELL NO!

I'm DeShawn Hatcher; I am a beauty expert, makeup artist, and author, My brand is honesty and humor with an afro. What's your brand?

TRANSFERABLE SKILLS

transferable or transferrable?

What's a transferable skill? It is a skill that you may have in one field that can also be used in a different field. Before I became a makeup artist, I was in corporate America, I worked as a portfolio administrator for an international bank.

My job was to:

- deal with clients,
- be personable,
- be empathic when they lost money on their account,
- deal with a boss that may not have been having a good day, etc.
- get coffee

Sounds like a makeup artist assistant, doesn't it?

Those skills transferred over to being an assistant, and so can your skills. Transferable skills take on many forms. I don't want you to think that you can't fit in unless you have a ton of makeup or hair skills. I keep saying it; there is more to this industry and then just makeup and hair skills. Figure out where your other skills transfer.

SET YOURSELF APART WITH TRENDS

Do you know what the hottest trends will be? I want you to research and follow the trends. I want you to understand the trends because it will help set you apart from other artists. For example, a few seasons ago, tribal was all the rage—it carried over into several seasons. If you could braid, you could work the red carpet, runway shows, and more. You could be one of the few assistants that were in demand, because not every hairstylist can braid. Do you understand? How can you fit into the trends? What if the next trend was designers using beautiful Asian models. Can you work on Asians? Then pull out all your work on Asian models, and make a nice presentation featuring them. Knowing the upcoming trends will allow you to focus your marketing on the next in-demand look. Trends go beyond lipsticks and hair. They can be anything in the range of fashion and beauty. Watch the trends and figure out how you can use them to your advantage.

"FAKE IT TILL YOU MAKE IT":
WHAT DOES IT REALLY MEAN?

"Faking it till you make it" is leaving the impression that you've been doing this job a long time, even if you really haven't. It's giving the perception of you being more seasoned than you actually are. When I assisted, I did everything asked of me with a smile, no matter how tired I was. I did the job well! I just thought "If the Key is OK, then my job is done." I was then rewarded by getting amazing references from Keys I assisted, and I got paid assisting jobs. I hadn't been assisting for long, either—this began to happen to me even on my first assisting assignment.

It doesn't matter how new you are; it matters how well you do the job. Opportunities happened because I made sure I presented my most professional side both on and off set, and you can too. My Key thought I had been an assistant for years. She was amazed it was my very first assisting gig. This is what I want for you, too. When you follow the rules of this book, it will give you the tools so you too can "fake it until you make it."

"Fake it till you make it" doesn't mean to lie on your resume, post fake photos, or fabricate your bio. It means to show up, be professional, do the job, and have people think you have been doing this for years.

LET YOU COME THROUGH

Assisting is a very personal job. You meet our kids; you are privy to our personal lives and their intimate details. That is one reason its such a hard job to get. Most artists want to get to know you slowly before deciding on choosing you to assist. Generic email introductions and mass cut-and-paste emails don't work anymore. Artists are longing for a more personal touch. If you can let your personality shine through in your marketing, you will be able to stand out. HOW? Stay in touch and stay genuine. Reach out with a personal note and an update once each month. Don't just include what you did, include how it made you feel. What did you learn? How can this help you in assisting them in the future? If you skipped the research in this book, you've skipped the whole reason for this book. A genuine connection will always outweigh one full of fake compliments.

TRUTH IN ADVERTISING

Please don't lie about anything. For me, this is the most annoying part of finding an assistant. When researching a potential assistant, I come across so many puffed-up bios and resumes, along with images from other artists without proper credit applied. Captionless backstage photos of artists strategically standing with a celebrity. The dumbest thing that I see repeatedly is photos with celebrities or photos of major events where artists claim to have worked, but no mention of those events on a resume or bio. FRAUD! We can see right through it all, and we do check. You are fooling no one but yourself, and you will not get the gig. You will be missing out on one of the most valuable positions this industry has to offer. At first, I'd get so annoyed with artists who practice this trickery, but now it just saddens me, because these artists don't understand that lying is not impressive. It is not the route you should take when seeking an assisting position, where one of the biggest requirement is to be able to trust your assistant. STOP LYING!

YOUR PROFESSIONAL OFF DUTY

For an artist, marketing yourself never ends. Even when you're home, you never know who you could run into just going to the corner store or the mall. YOU are your own advertisement. Your personal presentation is just as important as your on set presentation, and can speak volumes about who you are as an artist. We are all judged on our appearance (albeit unfairly), even off hours. We all know this to be true.

Just because you are off duty, doesn't mean you don't have an obligation to present yourself in the best light. If you do hair, please make sure your hair is in order. If you're a makeup artist, invest time in your personal makeup (clean and natural is fine.) I don't leave the house without a fresh face (my five-minute face and my Afro is always fluffed, lol). Why? I never know whom I could run into. First impressions are extremely important.

I live in Brooklyn, and yes, I do tend to bump into more people in the business. Even if you don't live in a major city, you still could be met someone who knows someone, who could be of service in your career. Your locale shouldn't stop you from presenting yourself neatly, even if you're just going to the corner store. Lastly, never leave home without your business cards. Always be prepared and professional. You are your business.

"Never oversell yourself. Be honest and up front about your level of experience."

JOHNNY LAVOY

THE RULE OF SEVEN

In advertising, they have this thing called the "rule of seven." On average, consumers must see an ad or product seven times before they buy. In our business, I feel like it's the rule of 25! It truly feels like it takes 25 tries before you can get a response. After all, you are selling yourself. Unlike in conventional advertising, our business is built on relationships and forming those relationships can take time. You've got to understand this, and not allow it to get to you. Think of it this way—if a stranger were to call you out of the blue and ask you for a job, what would you do? Wouldn't you want to know as much about them as you could? Remember, assisting positions are built on relationships.

YOUR FABULOUS FACE

I totally get it—I understand that we are in the generation of selfies, YouTube gurus, and makeup enthusiasts. If you want to work in this industry, however, business cards with your face or websites loaded with 25 different poses of makeup or hair you did on yourself do not qualify as professional.

Professionalism is throughout this book under several different scenarios, and why is that? You've got to understand that when seeking out assisting jobs, it's not about you. It is about the value you bring to your Key. A slip up in one of the major marketing areas, like presentation and self-promotion, can derail all of your hard work. Entering the beauty industry requires a standard level of professionalism and I'm going to keep repeating this point until it sticks. Keep your face off your cards and websites, this is not what is meant by self-promotion.

BLACKLISTED

Keys talk with one and another, and we let each other know when we have had a great assistant or a really bad assistant. The details of your poor performance will be conveyed to other Key artists, and you will not have any clue that this is going on. When Keys ask you who you assisted, we check if you're telling the truth. It's like any other job interview process; it is a reference. We need to know how well you can do the job. If you are a bad assistant, word will get around.

In today's more competitive makeup market, it is more important than ever to understand what an assistant does,

DESHAWN HATCHER

and what it can do for your career, as today's assistants become tomorrow's makeup influencers.

JAMES VINCENT

BE SOCIAL!

SOCIAL MEDIA AND MY MASSIVE PET PEEVES

Let me make this clear—FACEBOOK, INSTAGRAM, and YOUTUBE are not considered "professional" sites. Never send an Art Director, Agent, Booker, or Key who is looking for an established artist for paid work to any of these places. I do not hire anyone who tells me to go to their Facebook page. These pages may be fine for Bridal and more consumer-based services, but they are amateur when it comes to the professional world of print/editorial artists.

I question your professionalism if you direct me to your social media page. Are you a pro? Are you taking your career seriously? It doesn't matter how new you are, either. I'm sure you buy makeup and hair products, right? How about brushes? How about one of those fancy Zucca bags to carry your makeup? But my real question is, "Have you invested in your marketing and presentation?"

Don't sabotage yourself in the world of "free." You are in business, and being in business costs money. You must budget for purchases. By sending me to your Facebook page or Instagram, you're telling me that you can't afford a site. You're telling me, "I'm really not serious about being a professional."

Your presentation is important! This is an "image" business—is it not? You are trying to be a part of this business community—correct? There are rules you must follow. If you say you can't afford a site, which can be the cost of 3 Starbucks coffees per month, but you have 13 different red lipsticks in your kit, then please don't bother telling people you're a professional artist. You'll only do yourself (the industry as a whole) a disservice.

Now, I know you, you're going to be on social media—hell, I'm on social media and I'm not even that good at it. What makes social media such an amazing forum is that it's where you can connect to artists.

AGENCIES

When you are Key, more companies and even agencies are looking to your social media to see how many people "follow" you. The more popular you are, the more exposure you have for their firm. When you're an assistant, social media is no replacement for a website or a full marketing plan—it is a simple appendage. But remember that anything that can be seen by a professional should stay professional.

We may get your request for assisting, and before we contact you, we may check all of your social media. If we find questionable, unprofessional material, you may not get past this checkpoint and not hear from us. No one wants an assistant who doesn't know that you shouldn't upload inappropriate photos to social media.

NETWORKING

If you're introverted like me, or even if you're not, here are a few tips:

* You know how they say "work the room"? I don't. Instead of approaching people with, "What can you do for me?", I like to find out more about the person. Being genuine and interested in the conversation makes for a better evening then a race to hand out cards.

* I never approach anyone with an ounce of desperation—or lead with my card before I say "hello". Believe me, people can feel your desperation, and honestly, it's not a good way to try to network.

* Feel the room. Relax and just have a lovely conversation. If it is a networking event, you are there to meet people, and they are expecting strangers to approach them. You should, too.

* You are not bound to just networking events, because you will meet people all the time, everywhere. The minute you say "I'm a makeup artist or hairstylist in fashion/editorial", they will be drawn to you.

* You also don't have to stay until they throw you out. Stay for at least an hour. Make an effort to meet at least 2-3 people and then make your exit if you're uncomfortable. Always say hello and thank you to the host.

* When someone inquires about what you do, say directly "I'm a makeup artist or hairstylist, and I work in editorials and beauty. I'm looking for a great artist to assist." There is nothing wrong saying it directly. I also really believe that what you put out into the universe will come back to you—with work and perseverance. Why else are you at this event?

* I want you to think positive when networking. You will meet some amazing people just by going to events. This is the most important thing you can do for your business, especially if you're a newbie or trying to find new business. Remember, assisting is all about personal connection. When you make a connection at a networking event, you have the opportunity to nurture it and parlay it into something beneficial.

- ✳ Remember, while networking, you are *part of* a conversation—you are not *the* conversation. Seriously, how many times have you been around someone who wouldn't shut the hell up? You could just pass out from the endless noise. Do you really want to be that person?

- ✳ MOST IMPORTANT! You must have all of your marketing material in order. It is imperative that you don't go out without your business cards and your website updated. You never know who you will meet. There's nothing worse than going to an event and having no cards.

- ✳ It is necessary for your career to meet new people who can further your career. For me, it works well just to be personable, be honest, and be professional. BUT don't forget to GO OUT!!!!!!

FOLLOW UP OR BE LEFT BEHIND

When you make a connection, please follow up immediately. The way networking works, you are to keep in touch and reach out to the various people you have met. I have told a newbie who reached out to me at an event to contact me with his or her info. Too often either they don't contact me at all, or they wait too long to contact me (out of sight, out of mind). I don't take my offer of time lightly, and I'm sure many of my fellow artists, don't either. We are baffled by the lack of initiative artists seem to exhibit.

I met a young lady recently, in Barnes and Noble. We spoke for a while; I liked her. She found out I was a makeup artist and said she would love to assist me. I gave her my card, and told her to reach out to me.

Two months later I got an email from her saying, "Hi, Remember me?" Ah, too late, sorry! I had a huge gig and thought she would have been a great additional assistant and could benefit from it. Ten days passed, then 20, 30, 50, and 60! She blew it. There are so many other amazing artists who will keep in touch with me and who wind up getting those experiences.

Don't waste our time. If an artist is nice enough to hand you their card, they are showing an interest in you. It is up to you to continue the conversation by reaching out and sending updates. Keep those lines of communication open.

"The new age
assistants are all about
capturing a moment
to prove that
they were there.
Instead of living in the
moment and gaining
great experience."

LACY REDWAY

05

PRESENTATION

This is where we talk about all those fun, glossy items that get our attention —our marketing material. This chapter not only covers business cards, comp cards, portfolios, and websites, but it is filled with strategies on ways to get started in the industry and ways to get unstuck. It will help guide you on a fabulous journey. It will give you better understanding of how to set yourself up for success for the rest of your career.

KEEP IT SIMPLE

My girl, the fabulous Judge Judy, has a book entitled "Keep it Simple, Stupid". (I always loved that title; it makes me laugh.) When talking about marketing, I totally agree with the Judge; simplicity is key.

Websites with all the bells and whistles displaying work that is mediocre screams amateur, no matter how flashy the site may be.

How about a portfolio tricked out with colors and graphics, filled with substandard work? Business cards that have your face on them—remember, what are you promoting?

You see, you've done all of this work on the outside, but what artists are looking for is, YOU, your talent. Commonalities in work, and an understanding of who you are is much more important. Poorly-written introductory letters, websites with photos of your face on them, or (even worse) the most inappropriate cold calling known to man...I've seen it all. It is not just about a business card; it's about your total presentation.

Your marketing material is paramount in your business, whether you are a newbie, a seasoned artist or a senior artist. Let me say, just because you're assisting doesn't mean you shouldn't practice professionalism or the highest form of marketing you can achieve. You need all the same things a senior artist has. In fact, it is important that you treat this as a business with all the correct tools early in your career. That way, when an opportunity comes your way, you will be ready. These items will be representing you long after you leave the room. They are the ones that speak for you when you aren't present. The people who hire will hire you for your work and personality, not for your face on your card.

Let's get started.

HOW TO USE YOUR CARDS

When starting out, keep your card simple, beautiful, impactful and elegant, with an image that makes a person want to keep your card. Use the best photos you have, that best represent what you do, but that also target the artists you want to assist. If your best photo is one of avant garde makeup, but your goal is to assist an artist who does clean to red carpet makeup, then find your best photos of clean makeup and use those. I want to keep you on a straight path to your end goals. You must target the artist's style. Your fuchsia lip with the rhinestones could be saying, "I don't know your style", and that can get you overlooked.

BUSINESS CARDS

Hair artists can have multiple looks on their business cards. What they do is prominent; you can clearly see the hair. For a makeup artist, it's all in the fine detail. When you put more than one photo on a business card, those pictures become smaller and lose their clarity. A business card is only 2 inches by 3.5 inches. Restraint must come into play here. I prefer one photo, whether you are a hairstylist or a makeup artist. It just keeps it simple and makes a profound statement. Let the image speak for itself.

Keep the information straightforward—name, title, phone, email, website and (if you must) your social media sites. To satisfy your craving to put more photos on your card, Moo.com allows you to print out multiple cards with different photo fronts, keeping your info the same on the backs. You can do this with many other printers as well. It's a great idea, so I wanted to pass it along.

COMP CARDS

Comp cards, short for "composite." Comp cards are for you to upload a few different images so people can see a range of your work. Look for printers that do Postcards, Comp cards, Zed Cards—all the same thing. For a comp card, here's where you can add one or two avante-garde photos. Again, another opportunity to stop people in their tracks when you present an amazing comp card!

They come in various sizes, from as small as 4x5" to 8x11" or larger. They cost anywhere from 50 cents each to more than $1 each. These are not to be passed out like business cards; these are for more strategic marketing. Give these only to industry folk, artists, photographers, and agents. Comp cards are what gets placed in the back of your portfolio so people who view your book, can take your comp card as a reminder of your meeting. Agencies keep your card on file.

Think about how you'll be sending these—they're more like a postcard. You can put the address on the actual card and just mail it. I always put mine into an envelope before mailing. I have four photos on my comp cards; one large one in the front and three smaller photos on the back. If you have before/after photos, use the afters. Show a range of your work, and (of course) only use the best images you have.

LEARN ABOUT PAPER

Take a trip to your local office supply store and get yourself familiar with different weights of paper. No one likes a flimsy business card. Many people now order their printed material online. When the printers say we print on a 60# (pound) paper, you'll know what that feels like, so that you can make an educated decision. Remember, you're in business for yourself, you must wear all the hats, and one of them just may be "graphic designer"! You'd better know what you are getting. Something as simple as knowing paper weights can save you a great deal of anxiety, time, and money.

MISREPRESENTATION

Don't start off by misrepresenting your skills with the stock photos the printers provide. This is a business; this *your* business. If you don't have your work to use, why do you think using someone else's work is appropriate? It isn't. It may be a stock photo, but a makeup artist and hairstylist were hired to do the work. If you don't have a photo, don't freak out! Use a standard card with your name and info on it. Choose a cool, legible font and nice colors to showcase your style. Don't use any other artist's work on any of your marketing materials—it's fraud! (Do I really have to add that?!)

HOW MANY?

When I was new, I didn't realize I would constantly be changing my cards, because I kept getting better images. Keep the quantity low (50 to 100), and if you need to reorder—well, congrats! Had I known about this in the beginning, I would not have ordered the 5000—yes, 5000, business cards for 100 bucks. You think it's a bargain, but then you just have 4,550 to throw out.

PROOF IT

When it comes to printers, they don't always get the colors right and in our business, that doesn't help. By getting a proof of your card before you place your order, you save time and money in the end. To ensure all goes well, you do have to follow the printer's guidelines for accepted file types. If you don't have access to graphic design software like Adobe Photoshop or Adobe Illustrator, you may need to find someone to help you with this.

THE COST

Cards have become so much more economical—especially cards with photos on them. Depending on the company, YOUR FIRST 250 CARDS CAN BE FREE, or as low as $25 for 50. Comp Cards vary according to size. For example, my cards are 9x6 and cost $1 each. Don't forget about postage. It all adds up.

"Self-promotion
is what you do
to get the job.
Not something
you do on the job."

DESHAWN HATCHER

06

PORTFOLIOS

DESHAWN HATCHER

LET'S TALK ABOUT PORTFOLIOS

WHEN SHOULD YOU PURCHASE?

You do need a book, but you do not have to purchase it at the beginning of your career. It depends on this: do you have ten photos to put into the book? If you don't, then you're not ready to buy a portfolio. What you *can* do in the meantime is save your money, and be at the ready to purchase your book when needed.

ASSISTING AND YOUR PORTFOLIO

HOW TO USE YOUR PORTFOLIO FOR YOUR ASSISTING

In general, books are to be tailored to what your Key does. If you know, they do beauty campaigns for Neutrogena, don't have just your avant garde, fuchsia eye, and purple lip makeup, or your tree branch hairstyles. Show them you know you can do something similar.

For all my corporate America people out there, think of the portfolio as your resume. In our world, we'd arrange our resume to fit the position we were applying for by changing keywords, by positioning and highlighting our attributes. For an assisting portfolio, you change the photos.

Agencies will want to see more of a variety of what you do. They're looking for how good your presentation is. They even look to see how well you keep you book and tears/photos. Are the tears in order? Are they neatly trimmed? Is the quality of the photos, and the quality of the teams you're working with up to par? How will they perceive your makeup and hair? How well-rounded are you as an artist? Are you diverse in style and models? As mentioned in the research section, you still must know the philosophy of the agency to arrange the book to their liking. If you don't, you will run the risk of not getting on their list.

LET'S TALK ABOUT PORTFOLIO EXTRAS

IT'S IN THE BAG - $$ the other expense
When you leave your book somewhere, and you will have to at some point, it should be left in its carrying bag, with your name and return address. The cost for these bags can be $75 and up. Remember, each book needs a bag.

OPTIONS- extra extra $$
Your portfolio should have a pocket placed on the inside back cover. It's the place to store your comp cards, resume, bio, and a few other pictures.

LABEL MAKER-$
Your name and address should appear on the inside front cover of your book—that way they know whose book it is and can return it. Be sure to print out a lovely label with your name, address, and number on it.

SAY YOUR NAME-$$$
In this case, get your name stamped on the front of the portfolio. The cost for custom logos makes the book go up in cost—something to think about. YOUR NAME must be imprinted/embossed on the front cover of your book.

THE PORTFOLIO QUESTION I'M ALWAYS ASKED

To answer the end all be all, question I get at least 100 times year, *DeShawn, Why, in this day of everything on-line, do I even need a portfolio?* As of the writing of this book in 2015, portfolios are still relevant.

It still is an industry standard among some agencies. Many require you to have a book when interviewing for a placement on the assistants list. YES, there is an interview. If you have no physical portfolio, you will be in danger of not getting on that interview list. Yes, many of the bigger agencies have switched to digital, but that doesn't mean they all have. The world doesn't center around NY and LA; there are other markets that use portfolios. If you want to get on that assisting list, you'd better have a book. If you are in doubt, refer to your list of agencies you researched and simply call them to confirm—Portfolio or Tablet?

Portfolios give the viewer a chance to see your work blown up, full color, without distortion. It's hard to hide mistakes when the photo is 11x14. I have seen agents pull out magnifying glasses to review work, so don't be fooled into listening to the lazy artist. YOU NEED A PORTFOLIO! Oh, and don't think that only artists are looking; photographers like to see books, too.

"My book is
11x17
and filled
with beauty,
it makes for
a bigger impact."

ANDREA SAMUELS

Ideally, you would approach a Key artist with some work. But you may have the problem that your school didn't provide you with photos, or you're self taught and just getting started. What can you do to get assisting jobs? Let's look at this logically, shall we? This is a visual business, correct? We all have to start from somewhere, right? I did, and it wasn't easy. Therefore, you must have photos of your work to show, no matter the level. How do you get your foot in the door with nothing to show? You can't (unless you know someone)!

Your work, no matter the level, must be represented. For me, in the very beginning, I showed a few of my before and after photos, as that's all I had. Yes, those fabulous photos that show how well you can do makeup and transform and correct facial issues. By showing those, I got a photographer friend of mine to do a shoot with me. I used the photos from my second shoot and showed those to more photographers. I then showed my new photos to Key artists, and I started to test and assist. From there, I moved on to paid testing, and then on to full out makeup artists.

You might say, "But DeShawn, I don't have a professional photographers, or real models, isn't that unprofessional?" NO, it isn't. Why? Because you are truly starting from nothing. Like I said, you have to show something. No one in this business, not even your friends, will shoot with you until you can prove you know what you're doing. That is why I thought of using my before and afters. If I had to wait until I convinced a photographer I was worthy of a shoot, I'd still be waiting. You've got to become proactive in this business.

Please do not compare your journey to more seasoned artists and think that that is where you are to start off. You are starting off at the right place — the beginning, and it all takes time. We don't expect someone who's just started out to have anything remotely close to what a professional artist would have. So relax, and enjoy the journey. If I can do it, you can too.!

Let me break this down for you—if you still don't believe me!

A rush to pro can cost, hire a professional photographer who shoots beauty/ editorial photography, to shoot your first few tests. In NY, it can start at $700 to hire a photographer, this does not include a model or styling, which will come at an additional cost. If you need help in hair or makeup, you will have to pay for that service as well. All in, the cost starts at $1,500 or more—yep, that's for one shoot. Make sure your techniques are worth this cost.

"When I hire an assistant, I check their work to make sure they have a similar style of hair and makeup artistry."

MONAE EVERETT

DON'T RULE OUT SCHOOLS

You can find photographers at schools. Look for colleges/universities specializing in photography. For me to recognize talent, I took the time to acclimate myself to great photographers by studying all the fashion magazines I could find. You must get to know what amazing photography is, and the different genres of the business, only then will you be able to recognize it in others.

A DESHAWN STORY

I found and met a mega-talented photographer from the School of Visual Arts here in NYC, Sarah McColgan. When I reached out to her, I already had a book and website. I found her work to be "editorial", and it just moved me. I was hooked. Her images said to me, "DeShawn, this photographer is fabulous! Do whatever it takes to work with her." I emailed her at least once a month. I happened to email her when her makeup artist canceled for the next test shoot, the very next day. I jumped at the chance to work with her. We began to work together on test shoots and moved on to editorials, ad campaigns and so much more.

Now, 13 years later, we both have come up in this industry together, working on fashion editorials, catalogs, videos, etc. She's my sister from another mother. She's an MTV-nominated video director, has crazy fashion and beauty editorials, covers, and celebrities under her name. I'm proud to be her family.

Don't rule out schools, but do learn to recognize talent when you see it. Where do you think the next Richard Avedon, Herb Ritts, Dave LaChappelle could be coming from? Not everyone will be a Steven Meisel, but even Steven had to start somewhere.

HOW TO ORGANIZE YOUR BOOK

Out of all your photos, which will you choose? If you are experienced, 30 photos is the max, double page count as one. I know I've just gutted you. This process is painful. When you look at those photos, all you see is all your hard work, the hours you got up and went to set in bad weather conditions, dealt with rude models, and so much more. These are not just photos, they're your blood, sweat, and tears. Now I am asking you to discard maybe half, when all you want to do is hold on to them for dear life and fill your book up with all of them.

I feel your pain. I have gone through this process, and it was like giving up a kidney. Ah, but, we all need to do it at some time in our careers. Here's how you will decide. You will have to refer to your research. See, you didn't fill out all those forms for nothing. This is how your research will help to inform your decisions. If you're new, it can set you on the right path for the rest of your career, and if you're seasoned, it can help guide you on to greater success.

FOR MY SEASONED ARTISTS, HOW TO TAILOR YOUR BOOK FOR AN AGENCY

Let's look at this logically. If you're going for an assisting job with an agency that deals with more beauty than fashion spreads, then you know what? YES! You should pull from your assortment of beauty images.

Now, let's take this further. If the agency has more avant garde beauty (*Italian Vogue, Pop Magazine*) in their artists' portfolio, then you would organize your book with 60% avant garde, and 40% clean. You still want to show diversity and a range of skills.

You can even throw in one or two fashion spreads to show you have worked on location, or with a team. Of course, they must be of the highest form of editorial quality. It's another layer of what you can do. Do you see how your research can help? Remeber agencies have their own style you must fit in to.

FOR THE FABULOUS NEWBIE WITH NOTHING - YOU HAVE TWO CHOICES

1) When your beginning to test or when shooting your own photos, you can decide to start shooting your artistry toward the artists' styles you admire. If they do beautiful *Allure*-type shoots, you can begin to work your way closer to that style.

or,

2) You can tailor your search for assisting gigs that are geared toward your style of makeup or hair. Since you are starting from scratch, you can decide how you'd like to start. Either way, you now have a starting point. Can I get an "Amen"?

HOW MANY PHOTOS BEFORE
I APPROACH AN ARTIST?

For a newbie, five is the magic number. They must be the best five photos you have. Whether they're test shoots, or before and afters. Clearly if you're seasoned, you have a lot of photos.

IMPORTANT: Understand when shooting before and afters/testing, it can take 100 shots to get one good photo. It can take five photo shoots for you to get two great portfolio- or website-worthy photos. You must be discerning when choosing your photos. Don't become lazy and choose the first five you have. Accumulating great photos is a process that takes patience.

CONFUSED ABOUT WHAT TO PUT ON YOUR SITE/
BOOK? GET A CRITIQUE.

Whether or not you're just starting out, the question of what should you should put on your site and in your book can haunt you. Websites allow more flexibility and more photos than a portfolio, so they can soothe a lot of artists' fears. When you're first starting out, you will have only one category/one portfolio for your visitors see, and that is perfectly fine. I will keep saying, no matter the level of artist you are, your best photos must be on there. When you are a seasoned artist, you have a tendency to load up everything, and that's just as wrong. We've got to be selective and practice the art of restraint when dealing with our sites.

If you cannot be objective and remove or arrange your photos effectively, then you have to start seeking critiques of your work from Key artists before you begin asking for assisting gigs. You can also call agencies; many of them are willing to give critiques to artists. YOU MUST CALL and make an appointment. I still critique many artists who reach out to me for help with their sites. I understand that it's a daunting and painful task. As artists, we feel the need to hold on to our work until the end of time, lol. We artists can become stuck and need outside guidance. Seek any help that you need!

industry-standard
PORTFOLIO

✳ Standard Size: 9x12" or 11x14"

✳ Photo prints: $4.50 per 11x14" print

✳ Acetate Sleeves: I like the top and bottom to be open

✳ Page inserts: I like black but white is just as lovely

✳ Cover color: Black

✳ Cover material: Leather ($245) or wax skin ($130).
Leather books are cool, but they don't last as long as
wax skin. This pricing is from The House of Portfolios in
NYC

✳ Average total cost: $400 (Yes, that's one book!)

BEFORE AND AFTERS

Set up your own shoot, and take some before and afters. You can do it yourself, or ask a student photographer for help. Or maybe one of your good friends who loves to take pictures and does it well can assist you. No, the photos will not be the same quality as a professional photographer, and they don't have to be. Can we be real here? These photos are first level, they are strictly for getting a lower-level assistant's gig or for getting a photographer to give you a break. These are for you to have something to show (in the very beginning of your career) when asked, "May I see your work?" These photos are not your break into *Vogue*. GET IT? Here we have an example:

- **MAKEUP:** Colorful makeup opens her eyes, and the color is wonderful for her hazel eyes. Lips outlined with a pencil to create fullness, bronzer added to warm up the skin, eyebrows lightened to put the emphasis on her eyes. Anna's skin was perfection; not much foundation needed. No false eyelashes were used for this shot.

- **HAIR:** Is current. It's today's less fuzzy, natural-looking hair, styled with a loose wave. When doing hair, you don't always have to do overly dramatic looks. Show range and show that you know the trends. Hair, is really driven by the trends. Stay current. If you don't, your work will look old before its time.

- **CLOTHES:** She's wearing her own clothes.

- When doing this process, don't rush. Have fun. Do the best you can, and remember, this is crucial to your career. Treat this process seriously. Find family and friends to help you. Remember, it can take 100 shots before you get the one you like, and that is very normal. When we shoot editorials, they can shoot 1,000 photos to get the one. So relax!

- **SHOW RANGE**: Instead of the same look on every model, think of her on the red carpet, working out, going on a date. All will require different techniques and application to achieve these looks.

PHOTOGRAPHER: JUAN ELIAS

HAIR: MAYELA VAZQUEZ

CONCEPT AND MAKEUP: DESHAWN HATCHER

ANNA

LA CHAUNE

DESHAWN HATCHER

Here is a second example: Remember to show diversity/range in your portfolio, not just having a black model and a white model. When you complete your first photo, use that as a guide as to what **not** to do to on the next one. If you used lashes last time, skip them this time. Ponytail on the first, next do beautiful waves. Instead of a model with big eyes, go for one with smaller eyes but perhaps an amazing mouth. That is how you begin to show your range and your skill. Keep finding models' with diverse facial features and hair types. Doing the same makeup and hair on everyone or the same type of model tells us that you're a one-note artist.

On the left, we have model LaChaune:

* **MAKEUP:** Her complexion has been transformed. The darkness under eyes is gone, her skin tone is even. Discoloration is gone and highlight added, keeping the face palette neutral. Cleaned and shaped brows, and added drama with a fun pair of lashes. Lips remained neutral with a slight shine.

* **HAIR:** There wasn't time to do her hair, so she brought with her this amazing wig that help set the tone for her makeup. Hair stylists, yes, the hair is important to you, but the whole picture must be perfect. Get yourself a makeup artist to help you. Note: The makeup doesn't fight with the hair color it blends in.

* **FILTERS AND RETOUCHING** When you're starting out I want you to be careful of retouching and filters. Remember we need to see your work. If an image is overly retouched or filtered we will pass it over--and think you could be trying to hide something. Let your work speak for you.

BTW—FULL DISCLOSURE HERE: Anna is a dear friend of mine who works in an office, and LaChaune,aka, Chaunie is my niece. We shot this in my house on a fun morning/afternoon. On Anna, I used my pro makeup products. For Chaunie's makeup, I used all drugstore brands.

**PHOTOGRAPHER
(AFTER ONLY): JUAN ELIAS
CONCEPT AND MAKEUP:
DESHAWN HATCHER**

07

WEBSITES

THE POWER OF YOUR SITE!

WHERE THE HELL IS YOUR SITE?

WHERE THE HELL IS YOUR SITE? No, really, where is it?

Times have changed, and having a website is much more important than having a portfolio. Yes, I said it. You cast a broader reach when having a website. Your book is something that is for the one-on-one experience, such as in an interview, while your website can be seen all over the world, 24 hours a day. A professional online presence is imperative if you're going to be a professional artist.

I keep asking this over and over, "Where the hell is your website?" As a Beauty Director for several major events throughout my career, one of my jobs besides being the Key/Designer is hiring the crew. As a decision-maker, my job is very difficult. WHY? Unprofessional makeup artists and hairstylists inundate me with emails, and they have nothing to show me. They apply for jobs listed as "paid" or for the "professional artist only", yet they don't have a site. Does this make any sense to you? Would you believe me if I said I was the world's greatest makeup artist, but had nothing to show you? NO, you would not. So how the heck can I even hire you, site unseen? (Every pun intended!) Oh, and I will not look at your obscure and unprofessional Facebook or Instagram page. Let's go over some of the rules for having a site and why it is vital, if you want to be considered a professional!

WHO SHOULD HAVE A WEBSITE?

Anyone who is trying to be a professional print artist in beauty and fashion, and anyone who is looking to assist professional print artists, needs a website. How else will the people that hire you know your skills? Newbies, please don't be intimidated. You may feel that your work isn't up to the standards you have been looking at on other sites. So what? You don't know what the decision-maker needs. They could be looking to see how well you can blend, or how much attention you pay to detail. Those essential traits in an assistant can outweigh a bunch of crappy editorial tears any day. Don't block people who are in the position to hire you. Hire you!

WEB MASTERS - YES, THAT'S YOU!

No matter if you hire someone to design and maintain your site for you, or you use a template, *you*, my dear, are the actual "webmaster." You are the sole person responsible for its content, and when there's an error, you are the one who will take the hit. You must stay on top of your site every day and update it often. It is why I love the "KISS" rule: "Keep it simple, stupid!" :)

A DESHAWN STORY

In my first year as a beauty makeup artist, I had assisted on an amazing shoot with makeup artist Sharon Gault and photographer extraordinaire David LaChapelle. Woohoo, jackpot! When the shoot was over, I was given permission by the Key to use my work/magazine tears from the shoot to promote myself. Woooo, and you know I did. I put those pages everywhere, always crediting Sharon as Key. It took several months for me to get the magazine. In the meantime, I had also begun working in a photography studio doing paid model testing.

I had a huge number of images on my site: well over 300 images, test, and editorials. You couldn't tell me nothing! I loved my site! Until I made it too big to manage; I made the mistake of changing my site (for the sixth time). I moved the images around, but I forgot to add the caption that read "Key: Sharon Gault" on all the pictures. I didn't realize that I had made that mistake, until I was bombarded with a whole lot of angry accusations, saying that I was a fraud and that I steal other artists' work. Some people in this business don't give anyone the benefit of the doubt. Nor will they alert you to mistakes; they will accuse you! Though it was unintentional, I knew I had made a horrible mistake, and I owned up to it publicly and privately. WHY? Because I was 100% responsible for my site. I had been careless; I didn't check to make sure all the information was correct.

I do not want this to happen to you, ever, my dears! Keeping the site simple and clean, with good design and limited structured content will help you keep your site mistake-free. Keep it simple, and you will keep your reputation intact. This experience showed me that there's no room for error when representing who you are. Remember, no matter whom you hire to build your site—you are the one responsible for it!

"I believe assisting is necessary for personal growth. It shows kindness, respect and maturity."

VIKKI STARR

BE STRATEGIC WHEN PUTTING TOGETHER YOUR SITE

When putting together your site, you have got to be strategic. Make categories that make sense to a Key. Do you have a lot of photos in one category? Then break it down into subcategories that make sense. Subcategories usually drop down when you place your cursor on the menu on your site.

Since we are all about beauty here, let's use that as an example. The initial category is BEAUTY. You have 40 photos.

MAKEUP ARTISTS

For example, you have a lot of smoky eyes, red lips, clean/neutral makeup and body painting. Under "Beauty" on your menu, you can create subcategories, like:

- Au Naturel (for clean makeup)
- Smokey Eye
- Give me Body (for body painting)

HAIRSTYLISTS

For example, you've got a ton of updos: wedding, retro, and various braids: from fishtails and plaits to twists. Under "Styles" on your main menu, add subcategories like:

- Beehives (for the retro looks),
- Wedding
- Twisted (a creative name for a subcategory featuring all types of braids)

Limit the images to the best you have, and if you're new, keep the number of images per sub category to five. Only senior artists have a lot of categories and photos on their site—it reflects their history.

Have 10-20 photos? No worries. You can create a horizontal site (they scroll from left to right) and place photos in order of your subcategories. There's a site for everyone even if you have 2 photos.

BIO AND RESUME SECTION: USE IT YOUR ADVANTAGE

Bio and Resume sections are there for you tell the truth (raise your hand) and nothing but the truth, so help you God! Use the Bio to explain your background. Are you new? Say so. Tell us what it is you can do for us. Are you willing to assist? What skills do you have that can translate to helping the Key on set? Are you looking to test? etc. Then put your number and email on there and send it out. I remember coming across a photographer's bio page. It stated, "I am a new photographer with two years' experience who shoots beauty and fashion. I am looking for opportunities to collaborate with makeup artists, hair stylists and fashion stylists, who takes their career seriously." He listed his credits, and that was it. I loved that. I found his site on point, honest and refreshing. He didn't try to trick the reader by listing a fluffed up version of his very narrow resume. He let his work, and his desire to collaborate with others, speak for him. Now he's doing quite well, with a lot of editorials, and celebrities under his belt. His new bio/resume has been changed to honestly reflect where he is today.

BEFORE AND AFTERS

Earlier in this book, I was discussing before and afters, and how that's how I got started. Well, if you have enough afters, you can have a wonderful site to showcase your work. It will also be a great site to send an artist to get critiques when you're first starting out. It shows that you understand the business and invested time and money into your business. YOU will appear more professional. Those fabulous afters photos will look so much better when you showcase them expertly, like an editorial artists less like a bridal artists.

KEEP IT SIMPLE

I know I've said this several times, but artists can spend so much money getting flashy sites with custom logos made, that they lose "site" that this is about their craft. They also make fancy sites too early in their careers.

Do you know how I know this? I did it. I had a flashy site that was slow to load. Oh, but it was cute—NOT. It made no sense because I had over 300 images and too many categories. I found out simplicity was what is needed. In this industry, decision-makers have little time to devote to looking sites. No one has a half an hour to look through your site. Keep the bio short and to the point. Remember, you will be marketing yourself to photographers and senior artists—not to your best friend. Keep it professional.

WHY I HATE THE WORDS "UNDER CONSTRUCTION" AND "COMING SOON"

Can I ask you a serious question? Why would you give out your card to a Key artist or a decision maker who can hire you, if your website is not fully up and running? Please do not be in such a rush to be an assistant that you pass out poor information. What does an unfinished website tell me? It tells me that you're not ready. It is the single most frustrating thing to have someone pass their card to me, and to take the time to visit their site, only to find the words "coming soon"—or nothing at all. Take the time to make sure all your marketing material is complete before you reach out to anyone. You can blow opportunities that you never knew you had. When this happens I do not *set aside* your card; I *discard* your card. So do others.

CONTENT NOT ACCEPTABLE

Your images should be of the highest quality. They should always have every component in place. The hair, nails, makeup, models, etc., should all be PERFECT. If they're not, then don't put them on your site. You don't want to put anything on your site that will distract the artist's eye away from your fabulous hair and makeup. So, bad nails, strange model positions, bad hair, bad makeup, bad photography, etc. *must not* be placed on your site.

ALSO, I can't believe I have to write this, but photos of yourself with makeup or hairstyles is totally unprofessional. This is not Instagram or Facebook—keep this style of marketing off your professional site.

GIVE THE ARTIST SPECIAL ACCESS

You've done your research, and now it's time to send out your info. Why not make it even easier for you to connect to artists? By creating a "CLIENT ACCESS" page, you can design a page to showcase work you know (through your research) that pertains to what the artists you are targeting DOES. If that artist is all about clean makeup—pull some of your best clean makeup images from your beauty and fashion pages and upload them to the private client access page. You have just saved them an incredible amount of time by directing them straight to the work that would interest them. If they want to see more, they still have access to your whole site.

You can even give them a cool password that means something to them. If it were me, it could be "love color" or just my name DeShawn. I want you to use every opportunity to connect. If your website provider doesn't have a client access page, you can still make one for them by creating a special page called "new work" or named something like "Love Color." You can still send them a direct link to the page. In your email, let them know you've created this page just for them, and let them know how long you intend to keep this page open. This is especially fabulous when you have made contact with them, and they are awaiting your info.

DO NOT RUSH YOUR SITE-BUILDING PROCESS—take your time and play with the site. Take advantage of the trials the proivders offer, and make sure all your questions are answered before paying for anything. If you're designing your own site, I highly recommend that you find a service provider which:

- has easy-to-understand site-building tools
- has a good FAQ
- has a good customer service rep or online help that you can call (find out how quickly they reply to your questions and what their customer service hours are (24 hours on-line chat)
- has a trial period, during which you can try their service for free for at least 14 days?
- builds sites that are compatible with all different viewing devices, such as iPhones and iPads, Android devices, PC or Apple, etc.

Lastly, don't forget about obtaining your domain name. What are you calling your site? Keep it simple. Note: I use godaddy.com. (And no, I'm not getting any kickbacks for saying so). Long cute names don't cut it--if your name is available I'd suggest using that.

Success is not achieved alone.

The most successful people realize the need for a right-hand person. Their sometimes unheralded work is often the most crucial,

DESHAWN HATCHER

and there is no greater person — it is a symbiotic relationship. They are the difference between thinking about greatness and actually achieving it.

MARIETTA CARTER NARCISSE

Success is liking yourself, liking what you do

and liking how you do it.

MAYA ANGELOU

CO
M
CAT

DESHAWN HATCHER

MUNION

ARE U TALKING TO ME?

COMMUNICATION IS KEY. You have got to know effective communication and how to use it to get your foot in the assisting door.

DESHAWN HATCHER

COLD CALLING

A cold call is when you're reaching out to someone you don't know, who is not expecting your call, to sell your service. I get several calls a year asking me if I need an assistant. I am sorry to say that the people who do call don't understand how to make a skilled phone call. It's time that you learn.

Think of your cold call as your first interview—an interview that you're initiating—because it is! Be the best that you can—be professional. Familiarity has no place on any call when inquiring about a job. I cannot stress using proper English enough, but what I'm talking about here is formal business speak. BTW, I am not referring to English spoken with an accent, I'm saying that Ebonics, slang or informal words have no place on this call. I polled over 30 artists and this is one of the top complaints I received.

Endless chatter is another issue they brought up. The conversation goes on and on, and the caller never seems to get the hint that they're on an interview. When I say, "OK, thanks for calling," they just keep talking. What impression do you think that gives? It tells me that you may do this when we're working, and that is a huge "NO". We are not friends, and we are not colleagues. In fact, I don't know you. You are on a business call, and you're calling to become an assistant, which means you are calling about a job—right? So what's up with all the chatter? Keep on track, make a script and follow the script, so you can keep yourself on topic and stop with the jabber.

SERIOUSLY, WHAT TIME IS IT? Why, oh why, do newbies/artists feel they can call anytime of the day or night to ask senior artist questions? Do not call any artist outside the normal working business hours, 9am to 6pm. Honestly, would you like to get a call at 11pm from someone wanting a job from you? I don't think so. Use not only common sense but common courtesy.

THE CALL

On the following pages are just a few examples of the many forms of calls I have received over the years.

"Hello,"

"Yeah, umm, I'd like to know, umm, how I can be your assistant."

"Oh, who is this?"

"Lisa."

"Well, Lisa, I appreciate you calling. I'm not looking for assistants right now, but you could email me your—"

"Dayum! OK, what's your email?"

"Oh, it's on my site—"

"Oh, you got a site?"

"Yes, I do, my email is DeShawnLovesMakeup—"

"Oh, how do you spell that?"

[end scene]

DESHAWN HATCHER

Now, do you see why I don't like phone calls. You know what that says, it says? "I don't know who you are. I saw something on you a while ago and decided to call you. I don't know what you do."

HOW TO SET UP A CALL
HOW TO SET UP A TIME FOR A ONE-ON-ONE CALL

If you want to reach out to an artist with a call, this is my tip for you. Send an email first. A simple short email that says:

Hello, my name is (put your whole name) and I'd like to set up a time to speak with you at your convenience in the next two weeks about being on your assistants list. I so admire your work on the (name a project they just worked on), and I'd love to have a chance to assist you. Here's my website (put your link here). Thank you for your time.

THAT'S IT. Then wait for a reply.

Two things can happen: you might get an email back saying that they will set up a time—yeah, or you might get nothing back. BUT at least you tried to reach out the more respectful way, and believe me that speaks volumes. An artist will remember you a lot more (in a negative way!) when you call at 11pm than if you reach out respectfully through email.

Next, put that person down in your journal. Remember you are keeping track of everything you do. Mark the response (even a non-response) with a date and keep it moving. Resend an email a month down the road, with an update of some of your new work. They could have been out of town or your email could have gotten marked as SPAM. You may also want to check their blog and see if they're swamped with work. You never know why someone doesn't respond. Many times it has nothing to do with you. Just move on to the next artist.

"Hello,"

"Is this DeShawn?"

"Yes, DeShawn speaking, how can help you?"

"Ohhhhhh my God girl, I didn't think you would answer! OMG! Stop the madness! Girlllllllllll, I want to be your assistant so bad; I just love you!"

"Thank you, you're sweet. I'm on set right now—"

"I have so much I want to say wait, wait a minute..."

"Like I said I'm on set right now..."

"Uh huh, but I—OMG wait!

"What's your name?"

"Denise."

"Well, Denise, I'm sorry, darling. Right now I'm not looking for assistants, but please email me with your website and info. I'll take look and contact you when I get a chance. I do appreciate you calling. I've got to—"

"Oh really? 'Cause I think if you just got to know me—look here—how about we get coffee?"

"Sorry, really again, feel free to email me make sure you put on there you spoke to me today—"

"OK, yeah, OK..."

"Gotta get to set now."

"Uh-huh wait a minute. Well you know if you're not looking for assistants can you tell me how you did this makeup look—you did with lips its all colorful, I'd really want to know the products you used and how you used them. Can you just tell me real quick?"

end scene

When I met *THE* Pat McGrath, I made a complete fool out of myself—wooooo! It was hilarious! Ask me one day and I'll tell you the whole embarrassing story. So believe me, I totally understand the excitement of girls like Denise, in the call on the left. But we (myself included!) have to remember to focus, to keep our composure, and to be as professional as possible when we are seeking employment.

KNOW WHY YOU ARE CALLING—KEEP IT CLEAR

Make up your mind—do you want to assist or do you want something else? The old bait switch calls are annoying as well. If you want a critique, ask for it and get off the phone. If you want to be an assistant, ask for it, and (you guessed it), get off the phone. When writing an email, have one goal in mind: is it assisting or a critique? You can always ask for the other later. This is not the supermarket of free information. If you approach an artist with respect and a direct question or request, you may get the help you seek.

SCRIPT IT AND STAY ON POINT

Perhaps you need to prepare a script of what you would say. It will keep you on point and allow you to concentrate. You can stick to the main points you want to know and obtain the information you need. *Please* have a pen and piece of paper handy, or have the phone ready to type in the info.

COLD CALLING AGENCIES

Cold calling an agency doesn't do much. You will probably get through to the receptionist. They will tell you the criteria for getting on the assisting list. It would be a rarity for you to get through to an agent. Remember to be polite and respectful, because you just may have to call that agency back. Don't burn bridges. A simple "Hello, my name is (say your whole name and what you do), and I'd like to know how to get on your assisting list for makeup artists/hair artists?" Then listen and do as you're told.

"Hello?"

"Hi! My name is Denice Shortt. May I speak with DeShawn Hatcher please?"

"Speaking."

"Hello, I'm a makeup artist and would love to know how I can get a place on your assisting list?"

HOW THE CONVERSATION SHOULD GO

SCENARIO 1

If the artist asks you a few more questions (like how long have you been a makeup artist, why you want to assist, who you've assisted, etc.), good for you. Be prepared to answer. Keep the answers short and to the point. Thank them, and offer to email them your website info ASAP.

SCENARIO 2

If the person on the other end of the phone says "Send me an email", then send them an email. Don't you dare ask them what their email is—it will be on their site. Asking for their email addres is a clear indication that you did not research them thoroughly. If you have their email address in front of you, you can confirm the email you have is the correct one. Thank them for their time and get off the phone.

SCENARIO 3

If they say they're not looking for any new assistants, thank them and move on. Make a note in your journal of the date and time you called, revisit in a few months. Send an email that day with your info anyway, and check back in a few months.

SCENARIO 4

If the artist answers and says they're on set, acknowledge what they said. Reply with, "Oh, I'm sorry, I didn't mean to interrupt your work." Offer to call back at a later time, or ask if they'd prefer an email. If they say call back at 9pm, then call back at 9pm. If they say "Email me", then do what they say—promptly! Thank them and hang up. Do not wait days, because out of sight is out of mind. You are not the only person calling them on that day.

CORE CONVERSATION

Below I have an example of a typical call you may receive, offering you your very first gig. It paraphrased from my first call from the super-talented Sharon Gault—Momma Makeup—asking me to assist. What I left out below is how I thought I was going to pass out, how my leg wouldn't stop shaking when I was talking to her, and how I screamed when I hung up.

Asking simple questions will give you great information into your Key and what can be expected. It is not an interrogation, nor a time to get makeup tricks, but a time to ask simple questions an assistant would ask of their Key. I am always leery when first-time assistants don't have any questions for me. No two Keys are alike; don't assume you know what to do.

THE FIRST ASSISTING CALL EVER COULD GO SOMETHING LIKE THIS:

Key Hi DeShawn! It's makeup artist Sharon Gault. I'm flying into NY tonight, and my assistant can't make it tomorrow. I got your email a while back about assisting. I saw your work—it's good. Can you assist me tomorrow?

Me Yes, I can! Thank you.

Key I'm working on an editorial. The makeup look is from the movie *Taxi Driver* with Robert Dinero. You know it right?

Me Yes, I do.
   Is there anything I can do for you before the shoot?

Key Sure. I could use some mood boards on the film.

Me **Oh, I don't know what that is.**

Key Just put together some copies of the makeup looks on a board for me. I need about ten different makeup references.

Me Of course, I can do that.

Key Just give me the receipt before we start, so I can reimburse you.

Me Will do. **What time do you need me?**

Key	You can meet me at my hotel and then from there we can go over to set. I'll be at the W in Soho. Meet me at 7 am.
Me	**Is there anything you need from me as your assistant?**
Key	I'm pretty laid back, but will need for you to make sure the table and my brushes are clean, maintain my kit for me, and some other things. I will show you before we start. It's a tight shoot, so just follow my lead and keep close to our area.
Me	I can do that. **Is there a dress code? Do I need to bring my kit?**
Key	No kit, and just dress in a black shirt, jeans, and comfy shoes.
Me	I will. Thank you so much for this opportunity. **Please know you can always give me direction. I'm a fast learner**
Key	Great to know. See you in the morning. I'll have more details after I speak with the photographer. We'll be going to the studio directly from the hotel.
Me	**Is there anything I can get you before we start—coffee, some juice?**
Key	No, they will have breakfast there.
Me	Fabulous, looking forward to it. **Oh, what studio are we going to?**
Key	David LaChapelle's. Feel free to call me if you have any questions.
Me	I will thanks again. See you at 7. (Pick my jaw up off the floor!)

You did the work, and for that, you deserve a happy dance.

FROM THIS SIMPLE CONVERSATION I LEARNED:

- **About the shoot:** It's an editorial/fashion shoot. YES! It's all about the movie *Taxi Driver*—HELLO!

- **About how to prepare:** My research assignment was to look up everything I could on Taxi Driver. I went to Barnes and Nobles that day and brought books on the movie *Taxi Driver*, and on 70's makeup. I found 20 makeup references. I then went across the street to Kinko's and made copies of all the pages for the boards and returned the books. (Remember, this was before the internet. Besides, those books cost me over $150, you'd better believe they were returned!) Next I went to Sam Flax, and brought the boards, and went home to prepare for my day.

- **About the day:** where and what time I was to meet her, and what to wear. (I was a half an hour early ready to start the day.)

- **About the Key:** I now know she likes her table, kit and brushes attended too. She seems laid back and cool. Remember I already reserached her.

- **About the photographer:** It's being shot by one of the top photographers in the world! I researched David LaChapelle, too.

This is a sample conversation, not a list of the top 50 questions you can ask. I want you just to open up a dialog with the person you'll be assisting. When you ask questions, you get answers that will give you information. Don't be afraid so speak up; don't be afraid to say you don't know what something is.

I didn't prolong the call and speak with Sharon like she's my friend. I didn't ask her a million questions. I was direct enough for her to give me direct answers. You will never know all that will happen that day, and believe your Key doesn't know either. Shoots will go as they go, and you can be at the ready to handle them when something changes. Be prepared, it will be a day you never forget, and one that can change the trajectory of your career. This day with Sharon changed mine!

"The Key,
head person in charge,
lead artist, your boss,
the one who hired you,
is the reason
you're on set!"

DESHAWN HATCHER

THE WRITE WAY

Did you know there are many forms of communications? What about a simple letter of introduction to an artist you'd like to work? Is that a form of marketing? Yes, it is! You're selling yourself, to have them consider you for an assisting gig. You are communicating your worth, assets and attributes. In this section we will explore everything written.

Normally introduction letters can read like a novel. You feel the need to tell the Key everything you think they should know about you in one email, and the letter goes on—and on—*ad nauseam*. How you come across in your email will affect how the Key receives you. If you're unprofessional and sloppy with writing, or cannot convey a clear thought, your request may go unanswered.

COVER LETTER

COVER LETTER VS. A LETTER OF INTRODUCTION

Back in the day, it was a "cover letter" you used to introduce yourself and skills. These would be a few paragraphs almost mirroring your resume, with certain career highlights. Nowadays, it's shorter "Letter of Introduction" that one uses. It's normally one or two paragraphs, short in description, and it's a "to the point" kind of letter. You will always state the following:

* Why you're contacting the person
* What you want
* What your qualifications are.

You also need to indicate:

* you understand who you are writing to
* you are grateful for their time.

The best approach is to describe your career in 3 sentences or less—concentrate on what you feel the person would be interested in reading. Stop asking for free makeup lessons and mentorships without putting in any effort. Start giving the right kind of information that will get you noticed.

Hello Ms. Hatcher,

I am Denise Knicole. I'm seeking a position as an assistant on your team.

I have seen your work over the years and recently saw your work on actress Lauren Velez, of Dexter. OMG, I loved the color combinations on the smokey eye you did. I, too, love using color. My understanding of color theory has helped me produce some eye and lip color combinations in my work as well. I also love to do undetectable basing; I am super proud of my skills in this area. As you said on your blog, "If the base isn't right, your makeup isn't."

I am a self-taught artist with three years' experience. I'm a multi-tasker and quick learner. I bring many skills to the table besides makeup. I am personable, can effectively deal with difficult people, and am super great at research, due to my ten years as an administrative assistant.

My portfolio, resume, and bio can be found on my website www.dkmmakeup.com. I know you are very busy, so I will check back with you in a few weeks if I haven't heard from you.

I appreciate your time and attention to this email. I am really looking forward to assisting you one day.

Sincerely,

Denise Austin Knicole
Makeup Artist
917-555-5555
dkxmmakeup.com

WHAT MAKES THIS INTRODUCTION EMAIL WORK?

1 **The salutation** was professional (not "Hey girl…").

2 **The body** of the email stated who you are and what you want,

3 it acknowledged what the artist does (you've done your research!),

4 it explained what you do, and tied it into what the Key artist does (back to your research!)

5 it demonstrated knowledge of the Key beyond her site (research!)

6 and it provided a little background info on yourself.

7 In the body you've also provided a link to your information,

8 explained that you have other skills to offer,

9 acknowledged the Key may be busy, (showing a bit of empathy, this is always appreciated!)

10 **In closing,** you thanked the Key for their time,

11 said you will follow up in few weeks (make sure you do!)

12 and included a nice sign off and signature

13 As an added bonus, nowhere in this email did it say the line we hate, "I can learn from you!"

Do you see all of that information I received without reading several pages? I understand, you think we need to know your whole reason for wanting to be an artist, but we don't. Save something for later, for your interview. Stay on point and tell us what we can expect from you.

The other issues I want you to avoid is the "cut and paste letter." There are no specifics included, just generalizations. It screams "I don't know what you do!" Let us know that you understand what we do and how you can be an asset to us. Reread the research forms and the chapter, it will most definitely help you.

Be sure to avoid saying, **"I want to assist so I can learn from you."** You're there to work, you are applying for an actual job, not a lesson.

This is where homework/research is crucial. A letter like the example will get you so much further than a generic "What can you do for me?" letter. Why? Because you show knowledge of self, the Key and an understanding of assisting. You have just passed the pack of thousands who do the same, tired thing. I want you all to be better than the norm. Come on, my fellow fab artists—don't you want to present the best side of you? Don't forget to show some personality. Letters can be personable, kind, funny and warm... and still be professional.

By the way, my mock letter cannot be duplicated because it requires you to know the history of the artist. In order to pull off a letter like this, you must do your homework. There is no cut and paste here.

Add a graphic of your real signature to the bottom of your email. If you don't know how, go to your email provider. Be sure to include your phone, website address, and your full name and business name.

AGENCY LETTER

Just as you researched the agency, you will search for commonalities between your skill and what you can bring to their agency. As the example letter is laid it out for you to approach an artist, you will do the same for an agency. If you skimp on this letter, you can blow an opportunity for you to get an interview, and get on the list. You are now armed with everything you need, all you have to do is *do it!*

SPELL AND GRAMMAR CHECK

We all have hit "send" when we should have re-read the document. I transpose letters all the time when I'm typing quickly, and it is so annoying when I realize this only after I have already hit "send". It causes me nothing but anxiety. So spell check, grammar check, and read it over to yourself. OK, I'm talking to myself, too. You may ask someone to help you proofread—great idea! We all can use some help! The bottom line is, the letter should be perfect when you hit "send".

FRUSTRATIONS: THE WAITING GAME

I know firsthand how sitting around and waiting for a Key to reply can be Nerve-wracking. That is why reaching out to numerous artists on a regular basis is needed. The more artists you reach, the more likely you are to get the job. So, don't you dare sit by the phone and wait! Go out there and keep reaching out. I made a decision when I first started, to cast a broad net to as many artists/photographers as I could. Either to get a much-needed critique, or to request the coveted assisting gig. I wrote on a daily basis. I wasn't just sitting and waiting for the one reply. I feel your pain, but know that if you do your research, you will be miles ahead of those who just flounder around aimlessly with no direction. It will allow you to send out your information to *many* instead of *one*.

We get 20 emails a week on assistant inquiries. Your message has to stand out. I don't like the standard email.

DESHAWN HATCHER

Offer me chocolate-covered gummy bears and I might keep your email.

ROSHAR

A WEEK IN A KEY'S LIFE
(AKA: WHY ARTISTS DON'T RETURN YOUR CALLS/EMAILS)

MONDAY

* 9am Call Time
* Location: 1 Hour Away
* Press junket with a celebrity
* Wrap time: 5pm—fabulous!

TUESDAY

* 5am Call Time
* Location: 1/2 Hour Away
* TV Spot with same celebrity
* Wrap time: 12 noon
* Afternoon and evening spent revamping my kit for tomorrow

WEDNESDAY

* New Client, 6am Call Time
* Location: 2 hours away (up at 3am to get ready)
* 10-page editorial spread
* Wrap time: Midnight
* Home by 2am

THURSDAY

* 9am Call Time
* Location: 45 Minutes Away
* One client, quick shoot
* Wrap Time: 1pm
* 2pm meeting with Photographer for next week's shoot
* Home by 7pm

FRIDAY

* 8am Call Time
* Location 2 hours away (up by 6am)
* Catalog on location, house in the Hamptons
* Wrap time: 8pm
* Home by 11pm

That is just one week in the life of a working artist. God forbid the artist has to travel by bus/plane/train to another shoot. On top of this, we face lost luggage, stolen makeup, hectic location, foul weather, lost passports... and you wonder why we don't return your emails right away!

DESHAWN HATCHER

SHOW SOME EMPATHY

Good or bad, these artists also have lives. They have to do the same things as everyone else: washing the laundry, parenting, house cleaning, walking the dog, taking care of a sick relative, dealing with tragedies and emergencies.... God forbid that they relax, hang with friends, check their Facebook for a laugh, bill their clients, sue their clients, work on their kits, research new jobs, etc. Can you see why we don't always return your email or phone calls? Touching base at least once a month will keep you in their minds.

FRUSTRATION IN WAITING
CHECK YOUR ATTITUDE AT THE DOOR

Keep yourself in check. Your time will come, and if you actually get acknowledged, that is the first step; you should be thrilled. If you don't get any responses, don't blow it by being overly eager or too aggressive, just wait and follow up. It may take months and several tries before you get a response. When you do, it still may take months, due to the artist's scheduling, to even have an initial conversation.

I got a phone call on my way to a gig once, and the person inquired why it took me so F*#$KING long to return her email. Wow, really? Do you think she ever heard from me? Just keep pushing forward, and do what has been laid out in this book

Obstacles
are placed in
our way to see

if what we want is worth fighting for.

UNKNOWN

DESHAWN HATCHER

PART 2

YO
GOT
G

DESHAWN HATCHER

U

THE

IG!

10

NOW WHAT?

CONGRATS - IT BEGINS NOW!

Over deliver! That's what Jack Welch, former CEO and Chairman of General Electric suggests to get ahead in business. If your boss asks you for a cup of coffee, it's not just enough these days to simply get that coffee. How fast can you do it, how accurate is it, and what's your attitude when you deliver? It all goes into being THE ONE who will be chosen for better assignments.

I agree! When you over deliver, it will come back to you in kind. Would you rather hire the kid who sat and ate donuts all day, who talked to everyone in the office and did not do his job? Wouldn't you rather the conscientious worker who knows her job well, executes flawlessly and can follow instructions? I had an assistant who rolled her eyes at me and refused when I asked her to go to Starbucks; she never assisted me again.

I was the over-deliver assistant. In return, I was referred to top artists to assist. I was offered the elusive paid assisting gigs very early in my career, and I was called upon to work on jobs that the Key felt confident I could do alone. I was also so fortunate to have mentors I could call upon when I needed additional guidance, and believe me, I needed the guidance! I over-delivered on what an assistant did, and that's how I "got the gig"!

Even though there's the word 'Artist' in your job title, you still have to treat it like any other job.

DESHAWN HATCHER

Show up on time (or earlier), know your role, you're there to 'Assist'!

NICK BAROSE

11

KEY PERSONALITIES

I wish I could tell you every single Key is nice and helpful, but, unfortunately, that just isn't the case! No two people are the same, so why would all Keys be? However, don't allow one bad experience to keep you from your goal of learning. Conversely, don't have one phenomenal experience and then assume that every job will go that way. Be prepared to work, no matter what your Key's personality or attitude is like.

This list will give you a heads-up on the funky little personalities you could come across on your journey of assisting, and how to best deal with them. Though there are many personalities and ways to handle them, these gems are from my personal experiences, and I'm glad I'm alive to share them with you.

DESHAWN HATCHER

THE EASY-GOING KEY

This Key can be very laid back, not full of detail or chores. Check in often, see if there is anything they need done above the usual. Just be an all-around good assistant. If he says it's cool, follow his lead. These types feel that we are all adults. They don't need to police you all day, nor do they feel the need for you to cater to them. They may think that you asked for the job and should know what to do. The only way you can get a feel for this Key is by having the "core conversation"; it's imperative for finding out what easy-going Keys' needs are. If you find your Key to be laid back, you'd better read this book again for a refresher.

THE JERK KEY

This Key seems to like to make your day miserable. They can be obnoxious, belligerent, and rude. They may yell, insult, and condescend to you, but you must not let this bring you down. You must stay the course and be the best assistant. My rule is never to take anything said to you in this environment to heart. This kind of aggression has nothing to do with you. Do your job and keep it moving! I've had to deal with this type a few times in my career. I'd tell myself, "I will not solve his behavior if I storm out or react in a similar fashion, so I will just keep working." The goal for me is to learn all I can, and I did.

THE SELF EFFICIENT OR HELPER KEY

They either help you with everything, micro-manage you or do it all them-selves. Unfortunately, they make you feel like your services are not needed. These types are controlling. It comes down to trust. Can I trust this assistant will not destroy my things, will they be able to take orders as given and execute instructions? In the past, I've had my kits destroyed by assistants who didn't close the caps on lotions, who didn't listen to instruction and ruined brushes and palettes. The destruction of our kits, and the careless manner our things can be treated, can make the Key a little leery of assistants. For some of us this need to control will go away once you have proven yourself capable, for others it may never stop. Just know this: doing your job, no matter how controlling this person may be, is essential to your later success as an artist!

THE TOO-MUCH-INFORMATION KEY

OK, this person tells you all of their personal business, to the point where it can make you uncomfortable. They talk about their sex life, personal lives, drugs—oy vey! You can try to change the conversation to the job, but sometimes these folks just keep on going. Just do the best job you can! The more you work you do, the less you may have to listen. Be empathic, and keep it moving. Then go home, and wash your ears out with soap!

THE THROW-YOU-UNDER-THE-BUS KEY

This Key is tricky, because he or she is a passive-aggressive personality.

A DESHAWN STORY

I'm working on set alongside the Key. The Key asked me to oil the bodies of the models. I did as asked. Then the photographer said he didn't want oil, "Please remove". I looked at the Key, and she nodded yes, so I removed it. The shoot was underway and then the Key said "Put the oil back on!" I was totally confused. I went to put the oil back on. I began, and then the photographer yelled, "HEY! Didn't I just say no f*&king oil?" I was mortified. The Key said, "Oh, sorry, she didn't listen to me the first time! It won't happen again." What? She used me to try and get out of the situation. She threw me under the bus and rolled over me. Assistant to Key is a relationship that should be built on trust; the "I got your back" kind. Clearly, she didn't have mine. After the shoot, she called me to assist her on several occasions. Needless to say, I never assisted her again.

For me, this kind of behavior is a deal breaker. Be careful of this type of person, because they can set you up for failure before your career even starts. With these people, actions speak much louder than words—pay attention! Remember, you are there to build your reputation as a great assistant, and you hope that the photographer will remember you as well. If you are required to do things that he or the client may not want, they will remember you. When you become Key, he may not want you on set. Don't allow anyone to sabotage your career before it gets off the ground.

DESHAWN HATCHER

THE THANK-GOD-I-FOUND-YOU KEY

You show up, and learned a lot. The Key is funny, helpful, endearing, and wonderful. I can tell you from my experience that I have come across more of these types than any of the others.

THE HE'S-NOT-THAT-INTO-YOU KEY

The Key is super friendly, and you instantly like them, and you feel they like you. They give praise throughout the day, and you are riding high. You redo kits, clean the table, wash brushes, etc. all day long. Ultimately you are SUPER ASSISTANT—take a bow. The day ends, they thank you profusely, and you think, "Wow, I did so well! They will be using me all the time!" You follow up with a thank you email (of course). You are looking forward to working with them again. BUT you never hear from them again. What went wrong? To be honest, you may have done nothing at all that bothered them. It just wasn't a match made in assisting heaven.

Some Keys are not loyal in terms of assistants. Some have too many assistants, and though you may have done a SUPER job, they prefer to work with others. This can happen, and if it does, know that you did all you could. Never take this personally. Review the rules in this book and see if you broke any of them. If you didn't, add the gig to your resume and just let this Key go off to "KeyLand." Move on.

THE REVERSAL-OF-FORTUNE KEY

This Key promises you pay—yeah, right? Read on.

A DESHAWN STORY

At the end of a very long, two-day shoot, I was told "OMG! DeShawn you did such a great job for me! I want to pay you!" I was so excited and honored. "No one gets paid," I thought to myself—wooo! I was told the gig paid $500, $250 for each day. Cha-ching! I was told to invoice the Key for pay, and of course, I did, that very night.

So excited, I waited for my first official assisting check to arrive. I waited 30 days, 60 days, and then 90 days. I called with a polite reminder. I'm still waiting to be paid for that job, lol. According to Judge Judy, if you don't get it in writing, then the offer doesn't exist. They know this, and that is why they can decide not to pay you. Be careful!

HOW TO HANDLE THE JERK KEY

I've assisted, hell, I've encountered, ALL types of personalities throughout my life, and I have found it's all in the way you handle the situation. I try to have as much empathy for a person I can muster. I don't fight jerk with jerk, because that never gets anywhere. Keep your head down and get through the day. Honestly, who said assisting is supposed to be a party? It *is* a job. No matter the personality, I was able to at least get through the day, and gather important career information. How? Well, I simply ignored their eccentricities and decided to treat the job like any other job. In other words, I ignored their crazy. A good assistant can get through the day, no matter who he or she is working with, even if it is "the jerk." These situations will also help you in the future when you deal with clients who are just as obnoxious. Believe me, you can get one of those at any time of your career, and DARLINGS, you will be prepared! We are in a service business and must learn how to handle all sorts of personalities, be they Keys or clients.

AGAIN, EMPATHY IS NEEDED

Many Key artists cannot afford to not work. They must make the bills at the end of the month. We have to work through adversity and trauma, sickness and tragedies. I have buried friends and then gone to work the next day. I always think of that whenever I encounter someone with a piss-poor attitude, and you should, too.

PLEASE AND THANK YOU

Whenever someone has a nasty attitude, I listen to what they are saying, not how they said it. As long as there are no racial/misogynist/sexist overtones, I'm good to go. For me, that has been a winning formula to get through a lot of tough times. Never take anything personally. What sounds rude to some may not feel like rude to others, it is very subjective. I will say, if you're sensitive, assisting may not be the right position for you. If you require a please and thank you after each request, look for other ways to learn! This industry is a business, things change in a heartbeat, and the pleasantries may get lost along the way.

DID YOU LEARN ANYTHING?

Another thing to think about after working with the Jerk type is this: did you learn anything? Though, "The Jerk" is correctly named, did that person try to show you some things, albeit in a condescending way? Were there moments in the day when you actually gained knowledge? Not every Key will take the time to show technique; they are on a job. You may not be getting paid; you must learn something for your time—even if you learn it the hard way. When I had the time, I always found a way for me to learn—from afar. You don't want to disturb the process by standing too close or asking makeup or technique questions. Find a convenient space for you to watch, and take mental notes. When the shoot is done, ask your questions.

TURN RUDENSS AROUND

I have had a conversation with difficult Keys as easily as with the perfect ones. I'd ask questions before every shoot—I'd have the core conversation. When working, I always checked on them during the day, and ask "Is everything OK? Is there anything I can do that hasn't been done? "If I have noticed rude behavior, I don't say, "Hey Idiot, Why were you so rude today?" I may say, "Was there something I could have done differently to make your day better?" A lot of times, they don't realize they're rude. I've received apologizes from Keys with horrible attitudes. How? All I did was ask, "I see you weren't happy with me today is there something I could have done better?" Normally I get "Oh DeShawn, I'm sorry! It's not you!" I don't pry, I just express my sympathies and move on. If they are still belligerent, Darling, move on—cause you know the person just isn't a good fit for you. Remember:

- Always keep the conversation polite and respectful, even if they don't reciprocate.

- You are not responsible for their bad attitude. As long as you do your job well, your Keys reactions to life have nothing to do with you.

- You have the right to never to work with them again. (Note: by doing your research, you may find some not-so-nice posts about some Keys, which could save you from a day of ridicule.)

Now get ready to assist and learn!

HOW TO HANDLE THE
REVERSAL-OF-FORTUNE KEY

When the Key says they are going to pay you, I found a fast way to remind them of their promise. I give them an invoice on the spot. Unfortunately, for me, it took me years to figure this out, but I am thrilled to pass this along to you. When someone offers to pay you on the spot, whip out your invoice booklet. (Just keep the booklet in your kit.) Quickly fill out the form and hand it over to your Key. The Key signs it, and you give them a copy, and you keep your copy for your records. It's not as fancy as a personal invoice from your computer, but it is a binding contract.

If you already have one of these trusty, cute little booklets, I'm so proud of you. By the way, if you wanted to spend a little extra money, you can get the booklets imprinted with your name address and other important info.

Here's what you should write on the invoice—and write it clearly:

* your name
* your address
* your phone number
* your social security or tax number
* the Key's whole name
* the Job name

* the Job date
* the Job location
* A description—assisted artist _____ (put their name down)
* Terms of payment: NET 30 or NET 60. (Industry norm is 30 days, but know that it can take longer. Just ask the Key.)

Sign it, have them sign it. Take a copy; and give them a copy. If they pay on the spot, you can ask if they'd like a receipt. Just mark it INVOICE "Paid."

Yes, there are apps for invoicing, but there is nothing like getting a signature while the Key is standing in front of you. Also, they can't claim to have never received your email.

Judge Judy would be proud!

DESHAWN HATCHER

12

BEFORE
THE GIG

...AND SO IT BEGINS: RULES TO LIVE BY!
IF YOU DON'T, YOU GONNA BE SORRY
Here's are some rules that you must adhere to before you get to set.

DESHAWN HATCHER

When I began to assist I was in my mid 30's, just out of corporate America. I wasn't a child; I was a mature woman who previously made a lot of money, wore business suits, and had a 9 to 5 job. Getting on the floor, lugging suitcases full of makeup, and being broke were not things I had ever imagined or wanted to do. When I decided to go after my dream of being a makeup artist, I realized quickly there were going to be some things I'd love, and a lot of thing I wouldn't. No matter, I did everything that was asked of me. I didn't complain, I didn't argue, and I didn't show how annoyed I was when I was, lol. I kept my attitude in check, and I did my job. When I assisted, my whole philosophy was that I cared more about the shoot and the Key's success than I did about taking care of my own needs. It was never about me, or what I didn't want to do. I was there to assist the Key, and by doing so, I learned a great deal that I still use today with my assistants.

If you are a person that totally understands the concept of teamwork, then this job is perfect for you. If you must be the star, the diva, if all eyes must be on you, and if getting coffee is beneath you, please don't waste your time looking for assisting gigs.

I never felt that I wasn't an important part of the crew. I simply knew my place, and my place was to make sure the Key was well taken care of. I did my work. The rules are there because you don't have the knowledge, skill level, and artistry the Key has. They're not there to make you feel lower or lesser than the Key. Know you are an invaluable member of the team, and at the head of that team is the Key. So listen to everything they say, and everything they don't say. Follow what is written here.

NEVER BE LATE!

In fact, be early. If you're shooting in the studio, being early is fine. There is always a studio manager. When I first started, I was so early, I'd be sitting on the curb waiting for the crew to arrive. Being on time is important, no matter the location.

RIDE TO LOCATION

You may be meeting the Key for a ride to the location. They may not tell you, but you could be meeting up with the crew as well. Again, you should always be early. As they say, "If you're on time, you're late." If you're late to the pick-up location, you could cause the whole shoot to be off schedule, and that is not the kind of issue you want hanging over you on set. You may be fired before you even get started.

As an assistant, I worked even when facing stomach viruses, bad knees, car accidents and many other issues. No one wants to hear any excuses about how bad you're feeling or why you're late. Get to set on time. If you are going to be delayed, call or text the Key immediately.

DRESS CODE

I had an assistant show up to set with sequence top and boots. It was a sequence explosion. Absolutely NO sequence on set! It's not a fashion show, and you are not Naomi Campbell on the runway. Leave that to the models and the stylist. You've never assisted and don't know what to wear? Wear a pair of dark jeans and a dark top (black top is preferable). Everything should be as clean as your kit (and your kit should be spotless). No holes in your jeans, and no dirty clothes! Be professional. Just subscribe to this very normal dress code, and you'll be good to go. What you cannot do is wear high heels/sandals/open-toe shoes; show excessive cleavage; or flaunt distracting tattoos, piercings, makeup or wild hair, unless approved by the Key. Keep your appearance neat, and do the job.

HYGIENE: YOUR FUNKINESS IS UNACCEPTABLE

I can't believe I have to put this in writing: don't come to work smelly. If you need to carry deodorant with you to ensure you smell fresh all day, please do so. To be on the safe side, always have mints in your pocket to ensure fresh breath. Remember, we are extremely close to our subjects, no need to breathe bad air on them. No dirty nails, no dirty hair...get the picture? Lastly, cologne and perfume shouldn't be worn—you could set off someone's allergies, like mine.

PRE-PRODUCTION

At times, there is pre-production work for you to do. Be aware you may have to pay for a few items, and of course, the Key will pay you back as soon as you get in. If they forget, remind them before work begins, to get it out of the way. Hand over the receipt and ask for payment. Do not let it slide—you must get your money! You're not an ATM; you're an assistant. Just be polite when reminding them, and do so in private.

MEALS

Your meal will be provided to you. Depending on the budget, it can be a gourmet meal or it can be pizza. Pack a lunch and snacks if you have dietary issues. Remember, you're working and you may not get a break right away.

CALL SHEET AND THE BIG "NO"

You may receive a call sheet listing when and where you need to arrive. Print it out, or write down the location and studio contact information just in case your phone dies. Map out how to get there by using either Mapquest, GPS, for cities with subways/buses try HOPSTOP.COM.

Here's the big NO! The Call Sheet contains the contact information of everyone on set. This information is standard; it is not and invitation to add these people to your phone list. It is not your chance to call/email anyone on the list when you get home.

Don't become one of those shady, backstabbing artists. Eager backstabbing assistants think they can get away with reaching out to others on the lists, but in the end, they do not. By doing this, you will burn bridges with your Key and any other person you may have contacted. Your Key will be contacted, not you.

When you do a great job, assistants can be rewarded by the Key. Keys love to pass on jobs they can't do to their assistants, and even get you more assisting gigs. But when you stab that person in the back, you run the risk of a bad reputation. Don't do it!

CANCELING

We all know things happen, and you may have to cancel. Do not wait until the last minute to let the Key know. By doing so, you can ruin the whole shoot. Canceling at the last minute will set you up for failure. If you know on Monday that there may be a chance you can't make it to set Thursday, let the Key know on Monday. Apologize and then cancel.

Do what is asked, be intuitive to your Key artist's needs, don't overstep your boundaries, never try to schmooze the client, speak very little,

be attentive, be open to constructive criticism and last but not least be pleasant and not overbearing.

VALENTE FRAZIER

THE WEATHER

Not every job is located in a cushy studio. Many shoots are outside in the heat, cold, rain, and snow. You have to be prepared for the elements. Dress according to your surroundings. Check the weather before leaving for work, and check with the Key to see if you need to bring any other kind of items like sunscreen, umbrellas, heat wraps, etc.

YOUR KIT

If you're asked to bring your kit—it had better be clean when you open it. No spillage, no loose powders no sparkles. No empty or heavily-used eyeshadows and blushes that should be replaced. Brushes clean! Sponges clean! Bag clean! Sounds like the Army, doesn't it? The dedication our fabulous armed soldiers have is what we need to emulate with our kits. Soldiers wouldn't dare leave without shoes shined; don't you leave with a dirty kit. Store your kit under the table until you receive further instructions.

PAY: IT DOES HAPPEN

If you have been offered a paid assisting job— congrats! I want you to get as much information about who to invoice before you get to set. The simple question of, "Who should I invoice?" is important, as well as, how much the pay will be. Some artists may pay you at the end of the shoot, some may want you to invoice them, and some will have you send the invoice directly to the client. That is why that question is so important. Knowing where your pay will be coming from is equally important. The contact information will more than likely be on the call sheet, confirm with the Key.

Sending out your invoice promptly is important, when you get home that evening or, if you have an app on your phone, you can invoice right after the shoot. Don't wait. If you know all the information in advance, you can ask the Key if you should bring your invoice with you. When working, make sure this is a conversation before you get on set, or at the very least before the shoot begins. Do not wait until the end of the day when everyone is rushing to leave.

Pay in this industry sucks, to be honest. It's a wait-to-get-paid system. Pay can take up to 30 days, or longer unless otherwise stated. Collecting pay will be your responsibility. Please read "Key Personalities" for more about pay.

"Assistants have reached out to the exact same photographers I have a long-time rapport with, asking to help build their portfolio. I think that's shady. Every photographer tells me when this happens."

TARYLL ATKINS

13

CODE OF ETHICS

DESHAWN HATCHER

WHAT'S A CODE OF ETHICS?

According to *Investopedia.com*, a "code of ethics" is a guide of principles designed to help professionals conduct business honestly and with integrity. In DeShawn terms, this code helps you to not be a shady assistant.

ASSISTANT CODE OF ETHICS

Here is the code you must live by as assistant. This is what Keys are looking for and require:

* **INTEGRITY:** truthfulness and honesty

* **COMPETENCE:** the knowledge and ability you need to do the job

* **CONFIDENTIALITY:** keep your mouth shut and your keyboard locked

* **PROFESSIONALISM:** you act in a professional manner when working

Seems pretty straightfoward, but you'd be amazed at how these simple codes become mangled, and abused by assistants. If you follow these codes, your career will go far beyond assisting. In the following pages, I've listed a few issues assistants don't fully understand and have explained them in ways you can understand. I'm straightforward, truthful and honest. In order for you to be successful, you must live and work by this code.

LEARN IT BEFORE YOU GET TO SET

When you're assisting, there are rules, and many will be spelled out loud and clear for you in the upcoming chapter. One rule is, "All work done on set belongs to the Key." It's a rule that has so many assistants upset, and it is a rule that you MUST practice. YES, even if you do all the work, you still get credited as the assistant only. You cannot claim any of the work as your own. It cannot be placed in your book or on your website. I can hear you, "WTF is this DeShawn?" I'm going to explain it to you so you can understand—notice I didn't say *like*, I said *understand*. Whether you are new or have been working for years, this rule applies to you.

EXAMPLE 1

So many artists who want to assist have been building their portfolios, and testing for so long that they don't know how to exit the "me zone" and get into the "assisting zone". When you are testing and building your book, you are the person in charge of exactly how the look should be—correct? In fact, I'm pretty sure if anyone told you they didn't like the look, you'd probably shut them down. CORRECT?

Now, lets jump to assisting. How do I put this gently?
YOU ARE NOT IN CHARGE!
YOU DO NOT HAVE ANY SAY ABOUT ANYTHING!
YOU MAKE NO DECISIONS!
YOU HAVE NO CLIENTS!
There, was that gentle enough :)

You may have done all the work that day, but the final say comes from your Key.

Where did you get your instruction? **THE KEY.**
Who hired you and brought you to set? **THE KEY.**
Who will have final say on set? **THE KEY.**

There are so many other variables that go into working a shoot than just the beauty, and the Key knows how to navigate it well—you do not. Keys have meetings, go over concepts, research looks, storyboard looks, confirm with stylists, and oversee the shoot. You, my dear, get assisting credits. What's that? You get to say proudly and place on your resume that you *assisted* Pat McGrath, Vogue Feb 2015 or Givenchy photographer Steven Meisel. THAT'S IT! And it should be enough because, after all, you're there to learn while working.

EXAMPLE 2

Let's say the Key said, "Do anything you want." You're thrilled; you do it, and you send the model off to set. You are beyond confident that they will love it. Suddenly you hear the photographers screaming, "WHAT THE HELL IS THIS??? THIS IS HORRIBLE!". You stand there mortified. Who do you think will get the blame for this? YOU? NO, not you, the Key. The Key is there to keep everything as it should be whether or not they pick up a brush. When things like this happen, it is the Key that must take the hit, not you. The rule is that anything that goes wrong with hair or makeup that day is the sole responsibility of the Key. Stop worrying about the "credit" and worry about you getting what you came there for, a learning experience and to do a great job assisting.

THE CLAIM GAME: DON'T BE PICKY

Don't be a "picky" assistant. What I mean by this is, don't run around telling people things like, "See that right there I did that lip!" "I put the lashes on; I curled her hair!" Don't go taking behind-the-scenes photos and posting photos on social media with captions telling everyone you were "working" , as if you are in charge.

When you are assisting, you should also be working on building your portfolio, and testing with your team. What you're getting from the set is invaluable, but not if you nitpick. There are too many things to learn: how to run your shoots better, set up your tables better, or how to improve techniques that could change the way you do your craft. The time you spent writing down what you did, or in being concerned about your portion of the shoot, is the time that could have been spent learning.

THE CLIENT GAME: DON'T DO IT

Assistants can turn into unscrupulous, greedy, sneaky, backstabbing individuals. They steal clients, by using any means necessary. They become ENTITLED to what the Key has, and they will lie and cheat to get it. If you don't believe me, have I got a story for you. In fact, many Keys will have stories for you! By doing client poaching, you create enemies for life. You burn bridges, and will create bad karma for yourself that will show up when you least expect it. I am going to give you the rules of client interaction. It is up to you to be respectful and appreciative of the opportunity the Key has given you.

You're on set; away from the Key and the client offers you a job. *You are just thrilled! You think to yourself, "Wow, I finally made it, I just got offered my first paid gig!" The one rule the client lays down is "Don't tell the Key." You accept his terms.*

The client approached you because he assumes a few things about you:

1. Your ego will be stroked by the offer.
2. You will keep this a secret from the Key.
3. You're not loyal to your Key.
4. You're desperate to branch out on your own.

Now the client knows that he can cut the rate that he would have paid the Key. A job paying $1,500 will now cost him $400. Once you're done, he probably will not be calling you again. Why? Because, though he saved money on this job, he does love working with the Key, and he simply could not afford her this time. He knows you're not going to say anything. He knows you are not loyal or trustworthy.

Here's what could have happened if you told the Key. The Key would have diplomatically talked to the client, and found out that the budget for the shoot was less than half of their day rate. The Key would probably negotiate a better price for YOU. They keep their client, you get a cool job, and the client is happy. Keys often give loyal and trustworthy assistants jobs.

If you think the Key will not find out, you're wrong. You will have to list the aforementioned job on your resume, and post photos on your site. You will have to answer to them, and that moment will not be pretty. What does NeNe say? "You can't win when you're dirty!" So true! You can't.

Now, if you still don't understand, let me break it down in terms you *can* understand. I'm going to flip the situation around a bit, follow me.

IMAGINE WITH ME...

THE "Key" is now YOU (Insert your name here).
The "Client" is now YOUR HUSBAND.
The Assistant is your BEST FRIEND.

(Do you get this so far? OK, I will proceed...)

1. Imagine your BEST FRIEND approaching your HUSBAND behind your back for a secret meeting, which will only stab you in the back. Is that cool? Hell NO!

2. How about your BEST FRIEND passing her card and trying to hook up with YOUR HUSBAND. IS THAT COOL?

3. YOUR HUSBAND, hooking up with your BEST FRIEND behind your back? Neither one of them tells you, and you find out later.

Would that be OK?

I'd say we have the makings of an episode of Jerry Springer.

QUESTION: WHEN IS IT OK FOR AN ASSISTANT TO...

* Speak to a client?
* Pass out their own cards to a client?
* Accept jobs from the client?
* Entertain an offer from a Key's client?
* Keep secerts from a Key?

ANSWER: IT IS NEVER OK! DO NOT DO IT!

I am very meticulous when choosing an assistant from my Ted Gibson Educational Program to assist me on shoots. My assistant has to be punctual, quick and must be able to anticipate my needs before I know what

DESHAWN HATCHER

I need. Most importantly, my assistant has to have great *energy!* They can be one of the most talented hairdressers in the world, but if the energy is not right I won't work with them again.

TED GIBSON

14

SET ETIQUETTE

YOU'RE HERE FOR A REASON

CONGRATS. YOU'RE HERE BECAUSE YOU GOT THE GIG!

I know you jumped to this chapter! Tsk tsk tsk. This book is written to give you a complete lesson on how to land that assisting job. I get you; you can't wait to see what the rules are. But if you don't do the homework, your results will be lacking. Don't blame me! I told you how to work this book. Now after you're done with this section, please go back and start from the beginning if you haven't. ;)

For those of you who came to this section the right way, I applaud you for doing what it takes to get that job! :) The beauty of this book is, if you do the research, it will make you not only a fabulous assistant, but an artist who will understand how this industry works. You will discover the intricacies of not only finding artists to assist, but finding photographers, stylists, hairstylists and makeup artists. You can actually take what you learn here and build an amazing Rolodex of team members. Ahhh, but if you jump ahead—it can all be lost.

READ ON MY FRIENDS, READ ON...

01

ARRIVAL

YOU HAVE ARRIVED

When you arrive, before the Key, the conversation with those already on set should be short and polite. Introduce yourself as the assistant to the Key. Find out where you need to go—and then go there. Don't wander around; don't try to make friends. Next, let the Key know you've arrived, either by text or call. Inquire if there are any new instructions. Store your kit under the table, until otherwise instructed. ☐

02

THE SET UP

IT'S NOT SEPHORA

When you're unpacking the Key's items, you must do so in a way that is orderly and neat. Have respect for their items. NO dipping your fingers into eyeshadows, no spraying hair spray. This is not Sephora, this is their kit and must be treated with respect. Inquire how they like their table and set bag arranged, and leave the items alone. ☐

03

MAKING CONNECTIONS

MAKING SOME GREAT CONNECTIONS—NOT!

You're there to assist, and assist only. These are not your clients, and you are not the lead artist. Be respectful—do not pass out your cards or run around the set gathering information. Don't be surprised if get fired on the spot if you're caught doing this—you were warned. (Code of Ethics) ☐

04

TOO MUCH TALK

At times, we can be on set together for 16 hours—yes, I said 16 hours. General chit chat will come up, BUT incessant talking, is a big NO! Keep the conversation light. Do less talking and more working. ☐

"A great assistant:
is always early,
is a great listener,
has got my back, and
doesn't self-promote
while working.
You've got to
crawl before
you walk, darling!"

UNIQUE LONDON

"You can learn from *every* makeup artist you come in contact with. Be open!"

JENNIFER JAMES

05

SOCIAL MEDIA

TWEETING, PICTURES, ETC.

You are not to take pictures of your shoot unless given permission from the Key. Do not tweet, Intsagram insta-anything! Some sets have strict confidentiality issues, and if you're sending out texts/images you could be jeopardizing the Key's reputation and the privacy of the shoot. ☐

07

SHHHHHHH!

INSIDE VOICE—SHHH!

OK, so you know how parents tell their kids to use their "inside voices", lol? That means to keep it down. So, no yelling across the set at the Key, no loud talking— just keep your voice at a normal (or below normal) volume. ☐

06

CONVERSATION

TALK TO THE KEY ONLY

There can be as few as four people, or as many as 30 people on set. Striking up friendly conversation with someone on set may throw off the dynamics of the shoot. You can say something that can inadvertently put your Key artist in a bad light.

EXAMPLE: You strike up a conversation with a woman you met at the coffee station. She, asks you what you feel about the shoot and you say —"Well, the Key thinks the clothes are awful, don't you?" She smiles and walks away. YOU have just insulted the Fashion stylists, and thrown your Key under the bus. Extraneous conversation is not needed. There will also be several other assistants on set (fashion and hair stylists, photographers). This is not the time to make friends, give your opinions, or share Key secrets. ☐

"I look for Assistants to be on top of everything so I can be a creative and get the job done.

TYMOTHE WALLACE

08
LUNCH

No one cares if you're vegetarian and only eat tree bark, or you wished the lunch had lasagna. Unless asked by the Key or Crew member taking lunch orders, please, keep it to yourself. Bring a lunch and snacks with you just in case. Catering can be a crap shoot; we never know what we're going to get. No one wants to hear you complain about the lack of vegetarian food or anything else. Believe me, a lot of the food choices aren't good for meat-eaters either. You cannot be picky when on set—if you are, bring your own food. □

10
GOT MAKEUP QUESTIONS?

Assisting is not a lesson in makeup/hair. Keep all beauty-related questions until after the shoot. If you have had discussions with the Key about wanting to learn a certain technique, the Key may actually give you instructions while doing it. If not, don't ask until the shoot is over. □

09
LEARN TO ANTICIPATE

At times you may be alone on set, and you've got to be able to think on your feet. No, you're not the "Key of the moment", but you should be able to figure out certain scenarios as they pop up. If the Key left to go to the bathroom and the table is a mess, clean the table. If someone starts to speak with you, just let them know that the Key will be back shortly. If the model needs more lip gloss, give her more lip gloss. If the models has fly-a-ways fix it. If they ask for powder on set and the Key is not there—go powder. Unless the Key instructs you to do absolutely nothing, be a little proactive. Just inform the Key what you did when they get back. Believe me, if the Key walks away from set at all, they have some trust that you won't screw up the shoot. There are times I don't leave the set even once, not even to go to the bathroom, because I can't leave the assistants alone. But if I do leave, they must be able to think on their feet. □

11

TOO CLOSE

DON'T STAND SO CLOSE TO ME

No, I'm not talking about the 1980's song by *The Police*. I'm talking about assistants wanting to see everything I'm doing. By standing so close to me, I can feel their breath on my neck. Step back, and don't crowd. Depending on the client, that kind of staring can make them feel self-conscious and mess up the rapport between the Key and the client. Remember this isn't a lesson—take a peek, and take a giant step back. ☐

13

CELLPHONE OFF

SILENCE

Turn off your cellphone, in fact, put your cellphone in your bag. You are there to work, not text when you get bored, not to go on social media when you're bored If the phone must be out put it on silent. Be professional at all times. ☐

12

DON'T GET TOO COMFY

STOP ASSISTING

This is your third time assisting this Key, but instead of doing everything listed here, you become a little lax and laid back. You stop cleaning the table unless asked, you talk about personal matters out loud in front of everyone, and you even start to walk away without informing the Key. This is unacceptable! Whether it is your first or 15th time you are to be a professional. If you are bored and disinterested, then perhaps you need to stop assisting. BUT don't be upset if her next gig is something you really wanted to do, and you don't get the call. Assisting isn't always a party. It's a job and should be treated as such. ☐

"Don't treat assisting like it's a personal makeup lesson. Whatever you pick up in knowledge and exposure is cherry. You're there to work, not pick my brain."

MONFIA MORTIS

14

DON'T WANDER

STAY IN SIGHT

Make sure the Key has something to eat and drink throughout the day. Interestingly, you have more freedom than the Key. You can walk away from the set, but the Key can't. Depending on the set, there could be a lot of models, and the Key will be stuck working. Always make sure you check on them and that you are in sight in case they need you. The Key should never wonder where you are, or have to yell across the floor for you. □

15

WE DIDN'T ASK YOU

OPINIONS NOT NEEDED

I find it interesting how an assistant feels compelled to tell me the color of eyeshadow I should use, or why and how I should apply the makeup. Your opinion isn't needed unless asked for. Keep your opinions to yourself. It's very distracting. I totally understand wanting to help, but all it does is make your Key look like they don't know what they're doing and you don't know your place. □

16

KEEP TO YOURSELF

DON'T ASSUME

I have been on sets where someone will walk over to me and start talking, and the assistant just starts joining the conversation. Don't assume you are "IN" on the conversation. You are not. Remove yourself from the area and give them their privacy. If there's anything that pertains to your job, the Key will definitely tell you. OH, and please don't ask what the conversation was about. □

17

PRO TERMS

LEARN THE ARTIST'S LANGUAGE

I never say foundation; I say Base. I don't use concealers; I use neutralizer. Learn the proper terminology of the Key and use it. Know what the artist likes and become accustomed to how they speak. For example, if they ask you for base and you don't know what that is, you could slow down the Key by spending time looking for something that is right in front of you. □

"Know your position. There are boundaries."

REGINALD DRUMMER

"The best artists
and assistants
are like waiters
in a fine restaurant.
You don't really
notice them, but
they're always there
right when you
need them."

MARY ERICKSON

DESHAWN HATCHER

18

FEET HURT?

STAND UP

If the Key isn't sitting, you shouldn't be either. Shoots are extremely long (8 hours and up) sometimes the Key doesn't sit down at all, and neither should you. ☐

20

NOT APPROPRIATE

KEEP IT TO YOURSELF

Don't come to set whining about your life or complaining about the business. Don't flash endless photos of your kids and your dog, etc. This is a place of business and as much as people seem to think anything goes on these sets, it does not. Honestly, get over it, 'cause we all have problems. Keep personal anything to yourself. ☐

19

KEEP TRACK

Unpack neatly and orderly, clean the tables, clean brushes, keep the Key on track. Remember where you put things. The Key should be able to ask for certain items and you should be able to hand those items to them like a fabulous surgical nurse. Each Key has a way they like their tables set up. Just ask if there's any way they like it to look and be maintained throughout the day. ☐

21

CLEANING

Proper cleaning will keep you and the Key healthy. Make sure there's a trash can or trash bag around. Wash your hands when you use the restroom. If you or the Key drops a brush, get a new one immediately and hand it to the Key. Clean and disinfect brush that dropped. Keep hand sanitizer close and use it often. If you practice proper hygiene and sanitation, you will be ahead of the flu game. ☐

22

YAWN!

VISUAL BOREDOM

Believe me, some sets can be boring. Some sets have great music, and even have DJs spinning live, but some can be deathly silent. Some sets can become slow, with not as much work as originally anticipated. You are never to appear bored out of your mind. Believe me, if you're bored, the Key is probably is as well.

You still have a job to do, so suck it up, and do it. Find work to do to be helpful to the Key. Sitting in a chair with that "Lord-I'm-so-bored-I-could-die" look isn't professional. Though I do feel your pain. □

24

DON'T WORRY, BE HAPPY

If you have a bad attitude or grouchy disposition, keep it to yourself. Present a positive attitude at all times. When something gets on my nerves, I pause, count to ten, and then I make sure to smile. No matter how annoying it can be on set (and it can get annoying!), you must be positive. □

23

OVER-DELIVER

LISTEN/FOLLOW THROUGH

Simply put, if the Key asks you to get an Iced Latte with 3 Equals, then get them an Iced Latte with 3 Equals. (Ha, ha, that's personal!) Whatever the Key is asking of you—please listen. Simply do what they ask in a timely manner, and you will make their day go so much smoother. The request may sound inane to you, but can truly help the Key tremendously. The smoother you make their day, the more you will learn, and you increase your chances of being called back. □

25

PERSONAL INFO

MAKING FRIENDS

Working with the client, you are to be friendly and cordial toward them. This is not the time to exchange in-depth stories of a childhood trauma. You are there to help the Key. This is not a social gathering for you; this is work. Just because the Key may be having a wonderful conversation, do not join in. Sometimes the relationship between Key and client could go back years. □

"Put down that dayum phone and get back to work!"

DESHAWN HATCHER

"Being an assistant opens doors that would otherwise take years to open. Being a great assistant is the beginning of an amazing career and amazing relationships."

D'ANGELO THOMPSON

26

WATCH YOUR LANGUAGE

When you're speaking on set, be aware that others are listening. If every other word you say is a curse word, that is not cool. Keep the language devoid of profanity. Be cognizant of who is around you. You don't have to be part of the Royal Family, but you should be able to answer others directly and politely. The Key is not your friend, where familiar conversation should be discussed. This is a job, keep it professional. □

27

IT'S OVER WHEN IT'S OVER

WHAT TIME IS IT?

I've asked many of my fellow Keys what their pet peeves are when dealing with assistants. This seemed to be on almost everyone's list: *do not ask the Key when the shoot will be over!* It is over when it is over. Never plan anything on a shoot day, no picking up the kids from school, no going to the bank, no errands. Make other arrangements, so you can concentrate on the job of assisting. You accepted the job, and the job will end when it does. □

28

SPEAK UP

ASK QUESTIONS

If you don't ask questions, how will you know? Never assume you know how to do anything. Each Key has their own style, so asking questions pertaining to the job is essential. As previously mentioned, I'm definitely not talking about makeup or hair instruction questions or product discussions. Ask questions like where you should stand on set, how they want the makeup touched up, etc. Not questions like, "When is lunch?" "What time is this over?", etc. □

Never show up to set overdressed with too much makeup on. You're there to work behind the scenes,

which often
entails getting
dirty and
being on your
feet all day.
Look cute, but
within reason.

JACKIE SANCHEZ

29

DON'T ARGUE

Never argue with the Key, or anyone on set. Wait for the shoot to be over and address the issues you may have with the Key. Do not deal on set with anyone who may have been disrespectful or unkind. Inform the Key of the situation (in private) let them handle it when they can. ☐

30

TREAT THE SET LIKE VEGAS

GOSSIP

On set you will hear all sorts of interesting information. You are never to discuss, tweet, or "insta" anything about what goes on behind the scenes. Treat the set like Vegas; what happens on set, stays on set. ☐

31

AIN'T MISBEHAVIN

ACTIN' A FOOL

I cannot lie—there will be people who work on set that may not be as professional as your Key. I have been on sets, and have been amazed at what I have seen. They may do everything wrong—that does not mean you are to follow their lead. Let them run around and act foolish. If you think that type of behavior is acceptable on all sets, you are mistaken. Stick to the rules and be professional. ☐

32

PRICE CHECK

Asking the Key how much they are making for the day is extremely inappropriate and—honestly—none of your business. Never ask the Key personal information, especially when on set. ☐

"Assisting in the beginning of my career was the best thing that could have ever happened to me."

YISELL SANTOS

33
THE STUDIO

The studio is amazing. Get to know where everything is, bathrooms, coffee bar, towels, etc. Any thing in the studio that needs to be changed the manager will do. It's not your job to fix things, open windows, etc.

THE PACE
It starts off relatively calm, you think, "Ahh, this is pretty cool". Then the pace picks up, sometimes to a manic speed. You've got to keep up. That's why the dress rules say "comfy shoes". You will be running all over set and you must do everything quickly. ☐

35
ON SET

Stand next to or behind the Key when on set. Alert them to things that look wrong. Make sure the set bag is completely stocked. Running back to the table to find the brush you should have had in the kit takes time. There is much to learn when you're on set. Soak up everything, from lighting to models poses. ☐

34
BE CAREFUL

The set itself can be made up of fake walls, props, fake backdrops, etc. You cannot assume leaning on a wall is a good idea. You could knock it down, and the shoot will have to stop and reset, and that is time and money wasted. Food is often a prop, and if you decide to eat the strawberries strategically placed on a table, you could have just delayed the shoot, 'cause you just ate the props. If you stay close to the Key, in the designated areas, you will never get into this type of problem. When you do, it's the most embarrassing thing that day. I know. ALSO stay away from Styling--it's not a store, do not touch anything. ☐

36
ERRANDS

Many times you will be sent out to run errands for the Key. No matter what the errand is, you are to do it quickly and precisely. Write down the request and items. This is not the time for you to make phone calls or take a cigarette break. You are to do the errand and come straight back. Bring the Key the receipt, and get back to work. Don't come back smelling of smoke of any kind. ☐

"Make yourself indispensable and a good Key will fast-track your career."

DIANE CARREIRO

When I started, to assist Keyvon Aucoin, I used to bring a book. He saw me reading in my down time, and because he was super cool, he joked "Oh yeah, you're

DESHAWN HATCHER

working", and that's when I realized, when you are on set, there's no such thing as 'down time'. You can clean brushes, organize, and be attentive.

NICK BAROSE

"Assisting top
hairstylists taught
me so much
more beyond
just hair.
It taught me how to
prepare for when
my time came
to be the Key."

LACY REDWAY

DESHAWN HATCHER

37
QUICK CHANGE

ON-SET CORRECTIONS

When on set, things happen very quickly, and makeup and hair changes are to be done in seconds, not minutes. This is not a salon where you have a lot of time for changes. If you have to powder or fix fly-aways, do it quickly and precisely. Then go back to stand next to the Key.

When the Key's doing correction, be at his or her side. Be ready to hold bobby pins, brushes, or hairspray. Always keep the set bag handy. ☐

38
SET BAG

You are in charge of the set bag as well as the table. It is up to you to know what's in there, and where it is. You are to keep it clean, organized and fully stocked at all times. The Key should be able to look inside the bag and find exactly what they're looking for. ☐

39
YOU'RE RESPONSIBLE

As an assistant, you are responsible for the all items. YES, that includes pencils, bobby pins, brushes, and more. Losing any of these items will surely get you bounced off the assistants list. I hate losing caps to my pencils. When my assistant lost four caps and a small palette, she was replaced. Treat the items with respect. You are to make sure everything that comes out of your Key's kit is returned in pristine condition. ☐

40

CELEBRITY SILENCE

CRICKETS

When dealing with celebrities, (whether they be photographers, actors, singers, creative directors etc.), you can experience this thing I call "crickets". It happened to me when I assisted, and it *will* happen to you.

"Crickets" is when you are introduced to the celebrity and they totally ignore you. You say hello, they say nothing. You say, nice to meet you, they say nothing. You help them throughout the day, they say nothing. Don't take it personally, just do your job. To them you are the "assistant of the moment" and therefore they don't feel the need to address you. It's rude, no doubt—but who cares, just do your job. □

41

ATTENTION!

BECOME AN E.R. NURSE

ER Nurses stand close to the doctor; they're able to anticipate what the doctor needs. They waste no time in handing them whatever they're asked for. That is what makes a great assistant, too. When working alongside the Key, you want things to go as smoothly as possible. You are there to assist; you're at the ready. The Key should not have to repeat requests. Slow responses to requests and lack of preparation are signs you're not doing your job well. □

42

DUPLICATION

If you are fortunate, the Key may feel you are ready to do touch ups/makeup on set. You must be able to recreate what has already been done. That is, this is not the time for you to put your own spin on what you feel the makeup/hair should be. Your task is to duplicate what the Key has left. Be aware of the style. Did they leave the model very powered, or not at all? Is the red lip a strong one or more of a stain? It's your job to put the model back to the way their makeup was originally created. □

"I realized assisting makeup artists was not about beating faces and leaving. It was about watching your work, making sure it's perfect."

CELINE MARTIN

43

MARTINI SHOT

THAT'S A WRAP

The shoot is coming to an end, and its time to pack up. Do not rush this job. In fact, toward the end of the shoot, ask the Key when they feel is a good time for you to start cleaning up. You can get a jump on getting their kits packed and in order. Don't forget the set bag items that are still being used. You can make yourself invaluable when you know when and how to pack up. You never want to clean up too soon, because you could inadvertently put something away they made need. By being proactive and showing that you are ready to help them get out as efficiently as possible and on time, you can only make yourself look good.

When you do pack up, make sure everything is sealed tightly and put away neatly. I cannot tell you how great my horror is when I open up my kit and see powder and liquid foundation all over the place. □

44

WHAT A LIST!

GOOD LORD, DESHAWN!

Yes, I know. If you think these are common sense, and I'm totally condescending, believe me, there are so many people who don't know. These are guidelines, each Key will have their own ways of doing things and it is your job to find out and excute flawlessly. It used to surprise me: artists applying for assisting gigs but not having the slightest idea how to go about it, or people not having common sense about how to act on set. Making the Keys day go smoothly, can only make your assisting a valuable asset to them. We all have to follow rules and the more informed we are as artists, the better we will be at our craft. That is why I always say ASSISTING RULES! □

15

AFTER THE GIG

In the words of Oscar winner Matthew McConanhey,

"Alright Alright Alright!"

You are finished, and just got home—totally elated (I hope).
Congratulations!

WHAT DID YOU LEARN?

WRITE IT DOWN

I'm not talking about makeup or hair techniques. I'm talking about sets protocols, how to deal with a client, how to deal with this Key, how to set up a table and set bags, or what it's like actally working on this set? You MUST write down everything you learned as soon as you get home while it is fresh. You can begin to apply what you learned to your journey as an artist.

Check back with the previous lists; the Code of Ethics, Before the Gig and Set Eitquette: Did you forget to do one of those items? I want you to think! It is impossible to walk away from a set and say you didn't learn anything. I would seriously question your powers of observation. Do not let any learning experience pass you by. A learning experience is not just a positive experience. If something negative happens and some mistakes were made, no worries! Make a note of them, and then work on them for the future. Keep your eyes and ears wide open! Listen way more then you speak! Soak up everything like a sponge, because one day you will be using it.

The gig is over and you've written down, but you haven't the slightest idea how the key veiwed your performance. ASK? Send the Key a quick email. Of course, thanking them is a must. Ask "how did I do?" Is there anything you feel I can do for you next time I assist you [hopefully)?" If you don't get an answer, keep in touch with the Key, with updates of what you've been doing at least once a month. Alternately, you can ask if the Key has five minutes at the end of the day on set, and ask then how you did.

TIME FOR AN UPDATE

You've done your job and you got a great review—fabulous! Time for an update! Get your email ready to send out to prospective artists you want to assist. In your updates, include the artist's name you've just assisted and some details that make it a more personal update. Instead of the very generic newsletters that seem to be going around these days individualizing your correspondence will go a long way to making a connection with the next artist you'd like to assist.

DON'T BELIEVE THE HYPE

DON'T TAKE ANYTHING PERSONALLY

The one thing I really try to stress is *please do not take anything personally,* not the negative and not the positive. It's really, great to get positive feedback BUT, if you begin to believe the hype, then you're doing yourself a disservice, because no one is perfect. This is a business built on personality, and no two personalities are created equal. You can get along with 99% of people and then "BAM" there's that one Key you can't win, no matter how great you think you are. It can send you home in tears (believe me, I know). It could have you question why you're doing this in the first place. Honey, that can be crushing to your ego, so don't believe the HYPE. Everything is a lesson; so learn from this.

THE CHOICE IS NOT YOURS

Being too picky about the types of assignments will definitely get you bounced off an assistants list. Always inquiring if its a celebrity shoot, only wanting to work when the Key has a very high-end shoot tells the Key that you're not really into assisting; you're into the glitz and glamour and not the work. You are there to make the Key's days run smoother, no matter the job.

YOU DON'T OWN THE KEY

Do not think you're the only person on their list, no matter how many times you've assisted. If the Key called you and asked you if you can assist, simply say YES or NO. I've had an assistant mad at me, after learning of a celebrity shoot, saying that I gave "her assisting job" to someone else. Uhhh, wrong! As my girlfriend Trudy would say, "Madness!" BTW, I offered the job to this assistant first; it was declined. I didn't tell her what the job was; I only needed to know if she was available; she said "No." I moved on to the next assistant.

The question is *"Can you assist?"*, NOT *"Can you assist me on this celebrity shoot with Madonna?"* This attitude of ENTITLEMENT is total nonsense. Getting possessive with the Key and feeling entitled to any job is a sure-fire way of getting bounced off the Key's list. I cannot stress this enough; we don't have to tell you what the job is when we call.

Many jobs are unpaid, and if you have worked with the Key on several jobs you may begin to feel resentment. If you do, stop assisting them and move on. Resentment and Entitlement are the two traits that can form a shady assistant.

YOUR NEXT DECISION

You've just completed your first few gigs—massive congrats! On to the next assisting gig—right? You have the right to gauge if you can afford to take the job or not. Asking if there's a budget is an acceptable questions-but know there may not be. No one is holding a gun to your head—you don't have to take it. BUT make up your mind quickly. YES, they will call others, that's chance you will have to take if you don't decide quickly.

EXAMPLE 1

MAKE UP YOUR MIND—QUICKLY

Key	Hi DeShawn, it's Sharon, Are you available Thursday?
You	I think so. I just have to check. Is there a assistant budget? Can you give me 10 minutes to call you back?
Key	Not Sure about the budget, but sure call me back in 10.
You	(Call back half an hour later) Hey Sharon, I sure can!
Key	Oh, sorry, got someone else! I found out there is a budget
You	OK. (You're super bummed.)

One of the first things a Key can do when they get the call for a job is to ensure that they have an assistant for the day. If you ask for 10 minutes to answer, then you have ten minutes. Remember, the Key does not have to tell you what the job is. In fact, they may not even know all the details when calling. They don't have time to wait; they have to fill the spot, sometimes within minutes. So if you are fortunate enough to have a Key agree to hold off on calling someone else for even 10 minutes, consider yourself lucky.

EXAMPLE 2

You've now assisted them a few times…

Key	HI DeShawn it's Sharon. Can you assist me on Thursday?
You	OMG, yes!
Key	Great. Put a hold on Thursday.
You	Will do.
Key	Fab, will be in touch with more details as I get them.

You got the call again, congrats! They asked you to put the day "on hold", which means you're holding the day for them. If you get another job offer for the same day, you can let the caller know that you're "on hold." They know that means you are unavailable. For you, it also means you've promised yourself to the assisting job. If the new job offer is something you cannot turn down, you must immediately let the Key know you're suddenly unavailable.

IT'S NOT ME—IT REALLY IS YOU

Not getting called back? Is this your first assisting gig or your fifth assisting gig? If this is the fifth time you've assisted someone, and you never hear back from anyone, then it could be you! If it's continual then you need to learn how to give yourself a self-assessment. In this business, there is no one who will tell you on a regular basis how you're doing. If you reach out to artists and you hear nothing back, they either could be busy or they could be busy trying to ignore you. You could have done something on set that warrants that kind of reaction. I have to be honest, there are some assistants I never want to see again-they were so horrible. Unfortunately, without the Keys observations you may not know the specifics of what went wrong. In corporate America we are reviewed yearly, as a freelancer you will have to do this for yourself. So many artists write to me after they assisted someone, "Oh, DeShawn, I never hear back from people I've assisted then! I don't know why!"

Then you must evaluate yourself and your performance with the help of this book. Go over all the Key points in Part Two. Did you stand too close, did you not clean the table, or did the Key reprimand you during the shoot? The reason why I am so detailed in this book, especially with the rules or etiquette portion, is because I want you to understand the ways of the set. Breaking anyone of those rules could lead you not to be asked back. Go over your actions and make sure you complied with the rules and regulations of set behavior. That's why rule one of this chapter, writing down the events and actions of the day as soon as you get home, is so important. You've got to remember, making sure the Key's day goes smoothly increases your chances of being asked back.

"Didn't you just tell me to not take anything personally, DeShawn?" Yes, I did, when it comes to Keys that can be obnoxious jerks, etc. But there are times a little self-reflection is of great benefit. So, if you find that throughout your journey, the same things keep happening (for example, you only assist once, you don't ever get asked back) then you may need to look inward. It is not a reflection of how horrible you are as a human being, it simply means that you may need to re-evaluate yourself and alter how you go about assisting. You have this book to help you figure out what went wrong, if anything.

DESHAWN HATCHER

POST-GIG SELF-ASSESSMENT FORM

Remember to fill this out as soon as you get home!

Were you on time?

☐ Yes ☐ No

Did you follow orders well?

☐ Yes ☐ No

Were you able to be intuitive to others' needs?

☐ Yes ☐ No

Was the Key helpful and patient? If not, how did you respond?

☐ Yes ☐ No

Did you follow all the rules in this book? Go over all the rules and check the ones that applies to this job. What besides the rules in this book happened?

Were there any surprises? How did you handle them? Was it easy or were you tense and nervous?

How did the Key greet you?

Did you follow what they wanted? Were their instructions easy or hard to follow? If they were hard to follow, write down why.

Write down all chores done, in order:

Did the Key have to show you how to do something several times?

☐ Yes ☐ No

Did the Key praise your work?

☐ Yes ☐ No

Did you have the core conversation? If so, what did you learn, and what would you have liked to have learned?
☐ Yes ☐ No

If you feel your day was perfect, how can you improve upon that?

Did the Key become upset with you during the shoot? If so, why?
☐ Yes ☐ No

If you feel you didn't react well to certain situations, what were they?

How could you be more aware in the future?

Now knowing what they were can you come up with several ways you could have handled them differently?

Did the Key fall into any of the key personalities described in this book? If so, which one? If they fit more then one, write down all that pertains to them.
☐ Yes ☐ No

WRITE TO THE KEY

Once you are done with your self evaluation, then (and only then) contact the Key with a review. Here are some important questions to email to the Key. Feel free to paraphrase.

"I only want to be a great assistant and I need feedback in order to ensure I learn from my experience with you.

* *Was there anything I could have done better to make your day easier?*

* *Did I execute what you needed in a timely manner?*

* *Was my attitude OK?"*

List any other questions you have for the Key here:

Write down the Key's answers here:

Please remember, some Keys don't feel comfortable giving bad news. That is why you must become self-aware, and open to your surroundings and the Key's emotions, rather then their words.

Always remember to thank the Key!

APPENDIX

DESHAWN HATCHER

FASHION SHOWS

FASHION WEEK

I decided to include this to help you understand what it takes to "be on a team" for Fashion Week (formerly "Mercedes-Benz Fashion Week" NYC/LONDON/PARIS/MILAN). This position is not an assisting position. Being on the "TEAM" you are there as an artist to execute the makeup and hair designs. There are 167 shows, produced each season Spring/Summer and Fall Winter, always forecasting the looks and trends for the upcoming season.

When I Key fashion shows and runway shows, I have always included assistants. Assistants duties: *Backstage set up and breakdown, keeping track of the models, and getting the models prepared before they get to the team. They help out the "team", keeping the tables clean and get drinks and supplies. They may do nails as well—if a manicurist isn't available. They help with the model line up powdering and blotting—just before the models hit the runway. They get the total experience of what it's like to work a show but they do not work on models.* Not all shows utilize assistants. I find them invaluable to help my team.

Perhaps reaching out to other Key artists/beauty sponsor and offering your service as assistants (list the responsibilities from above), will get you backstage.

YESTERDAY AND TODAY

These shows have changed dramatically in the last ten years. It used to be agency artists and a freelancer's gig; the designer would hire either a production company to help put together the "team" (hairstylists, makeup artists, stylists, dressers, etc.) If the designer has a relationship with an artist, they may reach out to them to help put together a portion of the show. Nowadays most of the backstage beauty are run by makeup and hair companies. If you're not affiliated with their brand, you will not be able to work the show.

HOW TO GET ON A TEAM

You must have actual work experience and a portfolio and website, along with your business cards, comp card and resume. If you're with an agency, that's a plus.

* Understand this is for pro artists only.

- These are paid positions-though sometimes insultingly low.

- You must be able to work quickly and concisely.

- You must be able to follow instructions both demo and from a chart

- You must be able to reproduce exactly what the Key has designed and demonstrated.

- Can you work on different ethnicities?

- Each model is to look exactly the same, with no deviations.

- Sometimes the design (though always stunning in its context) can be multi-leveled, requiring a lengthy process. Can you follow lengthy instruction?

- If you want to "work the tents" first, find out who the makeup and hair sponsors are, and for which designer. Call them and ask to speak with their PR Department. Ask what Key is working the show and how their company goes about assembling their teams.

- You can also contact the Key through email. In the case of Keys for any of the tent shows, it would be best to first contact their agencies and follow their instructions.

- For shows not within the tents, do a quick search on the designers previous shows. There you will be able to find the Keys. Remember your research this is no different. Follow the rules of this book, to make sure you introduce yourself and your skills properly. Most importantly, make a connection with the Key. This should be done months in advance.

- You must have all your marketing and communications on point. If any of this is subpar you will not be working the shows

- Did I say this is strictly for the most talented of artists, if you can't line eyes, do a ponytail, follow instructions please do not contact anyone.

- Resources: Vogue.com, Harpers Bazaar.com, WWD.com, STYLE.COM, Agencies Blogs, Artists Blogs and websites

WHAT TO EXPECT

High-end fashion shows require high-end talent. They are hectic and fast-paced. They remind me very much of an emergency room. One minute it's quiet, everything is taken care of; and then a twelve car pile-up comes in, and it gets crazy. Backstage can be intense: flashing bulbs, late models, fashion coordinators yelling, exhausted and late models, the press and media. You have to be able to deal with this. For some, it's pure sensory overload, and many find the pace is too manic. I live for it. If you have no skill level, offering your services as an "assistant" to the team may be able to get you backstage. Remember, if you have nothing to show, if you don't market yourself correctly or communicate effectively, you will not get into the tents. These shows are something to aspire to.

NATIONAL SHOWS

MONTANA, UTAH, OHIO, RHODE ISLAND, TENNESSEE, SAN ANTONIO, AND SAVANNAH:

What do they all have in common? They all have Fashion Week. Yes, almost every major and not major city now have their version of Fashion Week. Finding out is as simple as a search for Fashion Week in your chosen state. Contact them and see what are the requirements to be on the "team". Find out who the Keys are, and contact them. For these shows in many cases, local beauty establishments are used instead of cosmetic companies. Make appointments with the salon owners with your book, and let them know you are a serious candidate for their team. Fashion Week is just not in NYC/PARIS/MILAN anymore.

MALL FASHIONS SHOWS

Mall fashion shows are a wonderful way to begin your fashion show career. They are normally run by the store that's sponsoring them. For example, Macy's presents Guess Jeans. You could be hired by Macy's. Hiring for these shows can be slightly different. Sometimes they use a cosmetic company in store to do the makeup—so you'd have to work for the brand to work the show. Other times they reach out to agencies for artists. There could a chance the store hires freelancer. I'd say it could never hurt to ask to speak with the person in charge of either the special events or the fashion show coordinator, and inquire about being on the team. Please bring all proper creditals with you, book, cards, website is up-to-date and please dress appropraitely. You are still seeking a "job"--remember this. This work experience can lead to the larger fashions shows in major cities—so don't turn your nose up at mall shows.

PREVIOUS SEASON S/S 2015 OF NY FASHION WEEK

HAIRSTYLISTS KEYS (SPONSORS)

GUDIO
MARC JACOBS
CALVIN KLEIN
COACH (REDKEN)

ORLANDO PITA
OSCAR DE LA RENTA
CAROLINA HERRERA
DIANE VON FRUSTENBERG
(BIOSILK)

PETER GRAY
BADGLEY MISCHKA

PAUL HANLON
VERA WANG

EUGENE SOULEIMAN
DONNA KARAN (WELLA)

ODILE GILBERT (ALL KERASTASE)
THAKOON
ALTURZARRA
SUNO
JASON WU

PETER LINDBERGH
BAJA EAST

MAKEUP ARTISTS KEYS (SPONSORS)

PAT MCGRATH
ANNA SUI
TOMMY HILFIGER
DIANE VON FRUSTENBERG

UZO LEAD ARTISTS FOR NARS COSMETICS
TANYA TAYLOR

GUCCI WESTMAN
OSCAR DEL RENTA (REVLON)

DIANE KENDAL
TORY BURCH
CAROLINA HERRERA (MAC)

KABUKI
ZAC POSEN

TOM PECHEUX
DEREK LAM
ALTUZARRA
RALPH LAUREN

GRACE LEE
NANETTE LAPORE (MAYBELLINE)

YADIM
PETER SOM (MAYBELLINE)

VAL GARLAND (MAC)
MONIQUE L'HUILLIER
BCBG

POLLY OSMOND
HONOR (KEVYN AUCOIN)

In the 167 shows of the 2015 Spring/Summer shows listed here, you see out of just 26, there are repeat Keys for different shows, and even different sponsors. Keep that in mind. If you reach out to them in the wrong way you can blow many valuable opportunities. Do your homework and research all the shows sponsors. ALSO be aware there are many start-up designers who could use a hand during Fashion Week. Do a search for upcoming, emerging designers, fashion institutes & fashion colleges, and go by the local trendy boutiques and see what designers they carry. Those designer maybe headed to the tents. Don't forget legends of fashion, WWD and Vogue and CFDA, will let you know who the hottest young designers are.

AGENCY WORK

SIGNING ON WITH AN AGENCY
I WANT TO BE SIGNED TO AN AGENCY. CAN I DO THAT THROUGH ASSISTING?

Yes, and no. It all comes down to having a conversation with the agency. You've got to express your interest in the beginning, so that they are aware of your goals. During the interview process is a good time to inquire about being signed on. They will let you know if it's feasible. Some agencies are very small, and can't accommodate additional artists; this is something you should be aware of. That doesn't mean that they cannot pass along paid jobs to you. This is for seasoned artists who are professional and talented, not for newbies who don't have a portfolio or clients.

They will monitor your assisting, they will ask for a critique from the Keys to estimate how you're doing. Clearly, if you do poorly, don't expect to be signed to any agency. By poorly I mean having a bad attitude, lateness, and not following orders. If they give you a time frame of six months to a year, check in at the sixth-month mark, with your portfolio in hand. See if they feel you can go on their roster. If not, check back in another six months. Remember, while you're assisting you are testing and shooting your own editorials and building your own portfolio. You will be assisting amazing artists. If you are not observing everything and learning techniques that can elevate your level of artistry, you will not be signed. If your portfolio is weak in any area, you will not be signed. They're not going to sign you because you've been a long-term assistant. Your work has got to meet the standard of their agency. That is why knowing the agency's styles, as well as artists, will help you prepare not only to be on the assistants list, but one day be signed.

Also, if I can be totally real here, agencies want to know what's in it for them. It's not enough to sign a good makeup or hair person. Its about your clients, and in some cases, celebrity clients. The better your clients, the better you make their agency look and the more money they can make. All of this is factored in to you being placed on their roster.

PAY AND ASSISTING AGENCY ARTISTS

I UNDERSTAND ABOUT THE PAY, BUT WHAT ABOUT AGENCY ARTISTS?

When you're assisting agency artists, honestly, I do expect you to get paid, not every time. It depends on what that artist is working on. For instance, if it's an advertisement, there is normally a budget for an assistant. Editorials, however, are the lowest pay there is for an artist. Assistant pay on editorials normally doesn't happen. Initially, what the artist may do is test you out to see how well you do, to see if you're compatible. Once you've proven yourself, they normally start offering pay. I just want you to be aware that just because you're on an agency assisting list or assisting an artist from an agency, you don't always get the paid gigs. As I mentioned before, pay is at the discretion of the key and can vary greatly. Once you have assisted them a few times, you can inquire about an assisting budget. A simple "Hey, is there an assistant budget?" is all you need to say, besides "Thank you".

FIRST ASSISTANT

HOW DO I BECOME FIRST ASSISTANT?

When you're a First Assistant, you are considered the right-hand man/woman of the Key. The Key will bring you along on top shoots; you are the first assistant on fashion shows, and when they cannot make it to a job, they may pass that high paying job along to you. Being a First Assistant is only for *THE* Best artist with the best attitude. One who follows everything instructed, can execute looks flawlessly, and is trustworthy.

I am so fortunate to have quotes and insight in this book by former First Assistants. They are all amazing artists in their own right Lottie (Lotstar), Nick Barose, and Lacy Redway, just to name a few. Follow them on Instagram for an amazing look into the world of fashion, celebrities, red carpets and photo shoots! If you're fortunate enough to be a First Assistant, you'll be working on *THE* highest level of fashion shows, photo shoots, and advertisements. You will not only be getting paid, you'll be flown all over the world. Go to Le book.com - there they list all the Keys behind the beauty for advertisements you see around the world. How do you become a first assistant? By being the best. Sorry, but there are no short cuts to this position.

AS AN AGENCY ASSISTANT, HOW DO I GET FREE PRODUCTS FOR MY KIT?

I wanted to touch on gratis for assisting. You know, the free makeup or hair products you see your Keys are getting. When I first started, I might get assisting credits in magazines. Makeup companies would give products to assistants who got editorial credits, but unfortunately, nowadays that's not the case. Beauty companies are more interested in the Key artists who are working and promoting their business. They give to artists who have editorial credits, high-end blog/magazine write-ups, and red carpet work. Gratis, the free stuff, is for the artists who have become steady, visible Keys and not assistants. Don't expect free products when you're an assistant. Gratis todays is something that one aspires to. I don't want you to be bummed by this; I want you to be inspired, because when you do get gratis, you, my darlings, have made it! It means you have arrived! Do the Happy Dance!

So, stop asking the questions about free products for assistants. I want you guys to concentrate on other things, like building your business, marketing, technique, etc. There are plenty of companies that do give amazing discounts to artists of all levels. Start researching and utilizing those companies to build your kit, and stop looking for free products. Face Atelier is one company that gives amazing discounts to artists on all levels. Camera Ready Cosmetics is an online powerhouse of professional products which has an amazing sample program, as well as many great specials to help fill your kits. Hairstylists and makeup artists also have Ricky's, which offers discounts as long as you have a business card.

TESTING

"Testing" is what you do when building your portfolio to showcase your amazing talent. I wanted to share with you a simple rule I want you all to remember when testing.

OPEN UP DIALOG WITH THE PHOTOGRAPHER

I keep hearing "DeShawn, the photographer didn't listen to me, or the photographer shot it full length, but I really needed a beauty shot." The photographer isn't omnipotent, and he or she doesn't rule the test. But photographers are not mind readers, either. Testing is supposed to be a collaboration. If you simply sit there like a mute and blindly follow—then that is *your* problem. You must speak up. A simple 'Can I get a beauty shot of this look?" is all that you need to say.

I've worked with phenomenal photographers when who wanted to know what my what I envisioned for the shoot. That is what I want for all of you. A photographer wants to hear what you have to offer. Even if this is your very first shoot, there must be a discussion on what you need. Why? How else will you get what YOU need out of the shoot? If this isn't the case, you may not want to shoot with them.

When you're looking for photographers to test with, remember that it should be a partnership (with everyone: hair, makeup, stylists and the photographer.) Having a dialog with everyone on set is essential for you to get that great picture in the end. If you don't have a dialog with the photographer before the shoot, how will you know about their lighting, positioning of shots, and their vision? You must speak up!!! I do not mean walk into set as Diva Almighty, but be prepared to offer your concept and be able to collaborate with everyone on set. If there's no discussion before the shoot, you must bring tears or pictures of what you'd like to do. You've got to open your mouths people, or you will not get what you need!

PRACTICE MAKES PERFECT

You've assisted; THAT IS SPECTACULAR! You go home and then what? Please do not become a lazy artist after all you have just gone through to get the most sought-after job of assisting. Take full advantage of the situation. You must quickly practice what you have learned.

Practice makes perfect! Why do you think people say that? 'Cause it's true. Practice does make perfect, or at least help you perfect what you've just learned. I would ask newbie artists, "Have your practiced your makeup application today, this week, this month, this year?" only to be given a craptacular answer like, "Well I don't have anyone to work on." *Oy vey!* I hate that excuse. Are you the only person left on the planet? There's no one here for you to practice on? C'mon! Finding a model shouldn't be difficult. Ask your momma, your momma's momma, sister, sister-friends, co-workers, etc. They would be more than willing to step up and volunteer their lovely faces and heads of hair—especially on a Friday night.

Then I hear Excuse Number Two, "But DeShawn, they're not real models." *Oy vey* for the second time! When I hear that, I just want to scream. Guess what? They will probably be your best models. Why? Because if the person has acne, discoloration, uneven bone structure, etc., these are the people you want to practice on. Any artist should be able to work on a flawless canvas or a great head of hair—right? But how in the world will you get the opportunity to get to that point, if you don't perfect your skills?

When I first started to do makeup, I threw makeup parties. Girlfriends and co-workers would come to my apartment, and I'd do their makeup . I'd take some before and after pics (ah, there they are again) and PRACTICE. Create your own photo shoots. Not everything needs a professional photographer or a flawless high-cheeked-boned model. Create a book of your work, and place the before and afters that are not book/website worthy on one side. Then, for the other side, you can create a face chart or just describe your corrections, or the new look you created. You can also practice decreasing your application time, and become a faster artists by developing shortcuts. All information from these shoots will be invaluable.

So, my fab artists and stylists, the next time you assist, you will have another technique or skill that can be of help!

THESE AMAZING ARTISTS PROVIDED QUOTES TO ASSISTING RULES! THANK YOU ALL!

TED GIBSON *(TEDGIBSON.COM)*
CELEBRITY HAIRSTYLIST/ENTREPRENEUR/MOGUL
OWNER of TED GIBSON SALON & TED GIBSON ADVANCED ACADEMY (NYC)
CELEBRITY HAIRSTYLIST with JED ROOT AGENCY

LOTTIE *(LOTSTAR.COM)*
MAKEUP ARTIST, NYC/PARIS/MILAN FASHION SHOWS/
BEAUTY& FASHION EDITORIALS VOGUE, ASSISTANT TO PAT MCGRATH

JOHNNY LAVOY
CELEBRITY HAIR AND MAKEUP ARTIST
LEAD GLOBAL HAIR ARTIST for L'OREAL PARIS
TOUR HAIRSTYLISTS FOR TAYLOR SWIFT

CANDACE COREY *(CANDACECORY.COM)*
TV/CELEBRITY MAKEUP ARTIST/BEAUTY PRODUCT EXPERT
EDUCTAOR/CREATOR of THE MAKEUP ARTIST WORKSHOP

REGINALD DRUMMER
TV/PRINT & CELEBRITY HAIRSTYLISTS

NICK BAROSE *(EAMGMT.COM)*
CELEBRITY MAKEUP ARTIST
LUPITA N 'YONGO, ANNE HATHAWAY, BLAKE LIVELY
FORMER ASSISTANT TO KEVYN AUCOIN

VALENTE FRAZIER *(VALENTE FRAZIER.COM)*
EMMY AWARD WINNING CELEBRITY MAKEUP ARTIST- TYRA BANKS SHOW

TARYLL ATKINS *(ABTP.COM)*
AGENCY MAKEUP ARTIST FASHION/EDITORIAL PRINT

ROSHAR *(ROSHAR.COM)*
CONCEPTUAL/ RUNWAY/ EDITORIAL MAKEUP ARTIST
INTERNATIONAL EDUCATOR and forTHE WORKING ARTISTS COMPANY.COM

LACY REDWAY *(THE WALL GROUP.COM)*
HIGH END CELEBRITY/ EDITORIAL HAIR ARTIST RED CARPET

TYMOTHE WALLACE
CELEBRITY HAIRSTYLISTS ZENDAYA, BRANDY, KELLY ROWLAND...

VIKTORIJA BOWERS ADAMS *(VIKTORIJA BOWERS.COM)*
CONCEPTUAL, BEAUTY, EDITORIAL
RUNWAY CELEBRITY MAKEUP ARTIST

CELINE MARTIN
TV MAKEUP ARTIST, GOOD MORING AMERICA

SIAN RICHARDS *(LONDONBRUSHCOMPANY.COM)*
TV/FILM HAIR & MAKEUP ARTIST DEPARTMENT HEAD
OWNER/CREATOR of the LONDON BRUSH CO.

MONFIA MORTIS *(GLAMKITTI.COM)*
CELEBRITY MAKEUP ARTIST,
CREATOR of the GLAM KITTI
CREATOR & EDUCATOR for the FIVE STAR BEAUTY SEMINARS

ANDREA SAMUELS *(ANDREASAMUELSMAKEUP.COM)*
AGENCY MAKEUP ARTIST, BEAUTY, FASHION & EDITORIAL

JAMES VINCENT *(THEMAKEUPSHOW.COM)*
CELEBRITY MAKEUP ARTIST
DIRECTOR OF EDUCATION, THE MAKEUP SHOW

YISELL SANTOS *(YISELL SANTOS.BLOGSPOT. COM)*
MAKEUP ARTIST & AMAZING BLOGGER

D'ANGELO THOMPSON *(DANGELO THOMPSON.COM)*
EMMY-AWARD NOMINATED MAKEUP ARTISTS & EDUCATOR

MARY ERICKSON *(CAMERAREADYCOSMETIC.COM)*
TV/FILM/PRINT MAKEUP ARTIST
OWNER of CAMERA READY COSMETICS

JENNIFER JAMES *(JENNIFERJAMESBEAUTY.COM)*
MAKEUP ARTIST & AMAZING BLOGGER

DIANE CARRERIO *(DIANECARRERIO.COM)*
HIGH FASHION, BEAUTY EDITORIAL MAKEUP ARTIST

UNIQUE LONDON
TV & CELEBRITY MAKEUP ARTIST

VIKKI STARR
TV MAKEUP ARTIST/ BODY PAINTER & EDUCATOR

MARIETTA CARTER NARCISSE *(MARRIETTACARTERNARCISSE.COM)*
LEGENDARY FILM MAKEUP ARTIST, DEPARTMENT HEAD & KEY
CREATOR of the MAKEUP ARTIST PLANNER &
AUTHOR of ROLL SOUND, ROLLING SPEED…

JACKIE SANCHEZ *(AGENTOLIVER.COM)*
CELEBRITY/EDITORIAL MAKEUP ARTIST

MONAE EVERETT *(MONAEEVERETT.COM)*
HAIRSTYLIST/MAKEUP ARTIST/BLOGGER/VLOGGER

Thank you

Thank you for choosing *ASSISTING RULES!*
It is my absolute pleasure to be the one that
you came to for help! My wish for you is to
go on to amazing things as time goes by.

Don't forget that as an *ASSISTING RULES!*
reader, you also have exclusive access to more
information online at www.ASSISTINGRULES.com

Much success,

DeShawn

CPSIA information can be obtained at www.ICGtesting.com
Printed in the USA
LVOW05s1837230915

455127LV00021BA/553/P